C000151686

Freedom
After the
Sharks

Geoff Hudson-Searle

Matador
9 Priory Business Park,
Wistow Road, Kibworth Beauchamp,
Leicestershire. LE8 0RX
Tel: (+44) 116 279 2299
Fax: (+44) 116 279 2277
Email: books@troubador.co.uk
Web: www.troubador.co.uk/matador

ISBN 978 1783065 349 (Paperback)
978 1783065 356 (Hardback)

British Library Cataloguing in Publication Data.
A catalogue record for this book is available from the British Library.

Typeset in 11pt Aldine401 BT Roman by Troubador Publishing Ltd, Leicester, UK
Printed and bound in the UK by TJ International, Padstow, Cornwall

Matador is an imprint of Troubador Publishing Ltd

I would like to dedicate this book to my Grandmother and Grandfather and to my good friends. Without their love and support, the success of this journey – and the book – would not have been possible.

CONTENTS

CONTENTS

Preface

Geoffrey's skills and self-motivation gave him the drive, determination and tenacity to continue a journey through hardship to reach self-fulfillment and, ultimately, success. His book describes the life journey of a young man's heart and his desire to turn his dreams and vision into a business success.

"Freedom after the Sharks" shows how, even in a declining economy, a business can survive and even succeed. It covers some real-life experiences and offers some suggestions for dealing with problems and issues. It provides a guide to finding your way in the business world.

The book is suited to entrepreneurs who might not be sure of the path to take or who want to benefit from other people's mistakes and failures. Other audiences include middle management or junior executives who are looking for a fascinating life story of courage, drive and inspiration, as well as graduates and college students, who will find information that will help prepare them for their careers.

Prologue

E ach of us is, to some extent or other, a reflection of the experiences of our lives. However, whether and how we succeed is determined at least in part by how we cope with those experiences and what we learn from them. This is the story of a man who, despite a difficult family life and professional setbacks, developed the determination, drive and skills to create a successful business and a happy life.

CHAPTER ONE

A Child is Born

"Every child begins the world again."

– Henry David Thoreau

The family into which Geoffrey was born on 6 February 1967 in Winchester in the Hampshire Hills was already deeply damaged. The marriage of his parents, Serge and Kathleen, had been troubled virtually from the start, partly as a result of their very different upbringings.

Serge's mother, Annette, had been born in Katowice, Poland, in 1908, but she had spent much of her life in Paris. It was there that she met Serge's father, George. George, who was one of nine brothers, started his working life with the biscuit company Huntley & Palmers. He came to run their operations in England before being sent in the 1920s to set up and manage the firm's first French factory, located near Paris.

As World War II began to loom, George – who had always been a planner – bought a house in England. The young couple and their son, Serge, moved into that home when the war forced them to flee Paris in 1944.

George and Annette raised Serge with strong family values; they encouraged him to be ethical, moral and just, and to treat people the way he expected to be treated. They were able to provide a comfortable life for their son, and although he trained to be a dentist, he eventually decided to go into the business of retail management of a shoe store. His parents had hoped that Serge would become a professional such as a dentist, and they had provided him with every opportunity to follow that course, but they supported him in his decision to move into retail. Ultimately, their main hope was for their son to be happy.

Kathleen did not have such a loving and stable home life. She grew up in the Kennington district in London. Her father was away serving with the army. Her mother enjoyed romancing soldiers on leave, and she was not interested in raising her daughter. Eventually Kathleen was sent away to Lincolnshire to live with a couple. When the couple separated, the mother did not want to keep the child. So Kathleen – rejected first by her natural mother and then by her adopted mother – finally found a home with her adopted father.

The rejection and the deprivation took their toll on Kathleen. She grew up to be distrustful of people, and she was often angry and resentful about the unhappiness and difficulties she had suffered. But she also was very beautiful, and Serge fell in love with her and asked her to marry him only a few weeks after their first date.

Annette and George were not happy with the match. They knew their son could be impulsive – they had watched him give up a career in dentistry for one in retail. They recognized the problems in Kathleen's personality, and they believed that she was taking advantage of Serge's good nature, his love for her and his wealth. They offered Serge money and international travel if he would not marry Kathleen, but he angrily rejected their offer and went ahead with his plans.

He was not even deterred when he discovered that Kathleen was having an affair with another man while she was seeing him. Serge was determined that his love could make the marriage work, and he married Kathleen on 10th April 1949 – which was Annette and George's wedding anniversary.

The couple had a son, Stephen, who was eight years old when Geoffrey was born. Since they already had a boy, Serge and Kathleen wanted their second child to be a girl; they even had decided on the name Jennifer for their baby. They were not prepared for a boy, and they were disappointed to have another son.

After the baby was born, Serge went to his parents' house to bring them the news. His mother greeted him at the door with her usual huge smile and offer of tea and cake. Serge told her that he had news to share with both her and his father, so Annette called George in from the garden, where he was tending his tomato plants. George came inside, washed up and joined his wife, son and grandson, Stephen.

Naturally, George and Annette inquired after Kathleen, and Serge told them that he had come from the hospital, where Kathleen had just delivered a healthy baby boy. The grandparents were thrilled, but they sensed that Serge was not completely excited and happy with the news.

Finally, Serge explained that he and Kathleen had really wanted a girl. They had decorated the nursery in pink, and they had chosen the name Jennifer. George and Annette were surprised at Serge's reaction. They pointed out that the most important thing is to have a healthy child, regardless of gender.

Eventually, Serge saw the wisdom of what they were saying, but he was still a little uncertain about the name. Finally, he said, "You know, Geoff Hurst scored a hat trick last year in the England vs. Germany World Cup final. Perhaps we can call him Geoff."

Annette and George did not think much of naming their new grandson after a football player. Instead, they suggested the more formal Geoffrey as a good compromise, and Serge agreed. But when the time came to bring the baby home from the hospital, Serge knew he had to handle the issue of the name very carefully. Kathleen would not like it if she thought that Serge and his parents had conspired to choose a name without her – and Kathleen could be very emotional and easily angered.

Serge and Kathleen lived in a small town called Andover, near the home of Annette and George, who wanted to live close to their son and his family and to be part of their lives. As Serge drove toward Andover, he got more and more nervous, even clipping a curb on the road. Kathleen noticed that something was amiss, and she asked her husband what was wrong.

When he was within a few miles of home, Serge told Kathleen that he had gone to his parents' house to tell them the happy news of the baby's birth. Kathleen reminded him that the baby was a boy, not the girl they had wanted and expected. But Serge replied that they should be happy to have a healthy child.

Then he added, "I was watching a sports news interview with Geoff Hurst — you know, the man who scored three goals for England last year in the England vs. Germany final. He has become not just a sportsman, but a legend. Even the Queen wants to meet him. And I have been thinking. I know we wanted a girl and spent nine months selecting the name Jennifer, but perhaps we could use the name Geoff or Geoffrey."

Kathleen assumed immediately that her husband and his parents had chosen the name for the son she had just delivered, and she was angry about that. She said, "So Serge, you mean that your bloody mother thinks it's wonderful that

I have conceived a child and she has named the child — without me — Geoff or Geoffrey?"

Serge protested that it was he and not his parents who had decided on the name. "Kathleen, although we wanted a girl, we have brought a beautiful child into the world together, and we must have gratitude for this gift," he said. "I like the name, and this should not be dismissed."

Kathleen was furious, and she accused Serge of not thinking for himself and not being able to stand up to his parents. Finally, she said, "You can have your child and your chosen name. I should never have married you. Being married to you is like being married to the devil and his family."

When they arrived at their home, both Serge and Kathleen managed to put on a good face as they introduced their new son to his brother and to George and Annette, who were taking care of Stephen. But the smiling faces only covered up the deep unhappiness in Serge and Kathleen's marriage. Serious problems remained, even as the parents put Geoffrey into his new pink clothes and laid him down to sleep in his pink cot in his pink room.

Several months passed, but the tension between Serge and Kathleen and between Kathleen and her in-laws continued to grow. When Geoffrey was baptised in the local Catholic Church, Annette took control of naming the godmother and godfather. She decided on herself and George – a decision that was not pleasing to Kathleen.

Kathleen felt increasingly isolated by what she perceived as her difficult marriage and the constant influence of Annette and George on her husband. She had difficulty coping with both her active eight-year-old son, Stephen, and the new baby,

Geoffrey. She felt she had lost control of her life. But rather than seek support or help, she became increasingly argumentative – and she needed to be right in all of these arguments.

Because of the responsibilities of her home life, she could not get a part-time job or meet new people through a class or other activity, and she could not get out of the house for a cup of coffee or lunch with her friends. She had never been very much interested in keeping house and taking care of children; she wanted to travel and go out to nice restaurants and enjoy herself. So she became more and more unhappy. She fought with Serge, reminding him of the promises he had made when he asked her to marry him and declaring that he had not kept those promises. Serge, who believed that her anger and unhappiness stemmed from her difficult childhood and the fact that she had never had a good role model to show her how to be a proper wife and mother, was continually making excuses for her argumentative behaviour and her outbursts.

One day when Geoffrey was a few months old and Kathleen was feeling particularly trapped, she decided to put the baby in his pram and go for a walk. She thought it would be a good way to get out of the house for a little while and to be alone with her thoughts. Serge, who was trying to be solicitous of his wife's needs, offered to go along. They could walk by the river together, just the two of them, he suggested.

Kathleen, however, was not interested in a little romantic stroll. She exploded, saying, "Serge, you are always interfering in my life. I despise you. I have sacrificed everything, and for what? I am living a life of an inmate in prison. I will never forgive you – why don't you go live with your mother?"

Serge's efforts to defuse the situation only made things worse. Finally, he broke down in tears, saying, "I only wanted us to take a walk together, Kathleen."

Kathleen, who was now out of control with anger, opened the door of the house and screamed, "This is what I think of you and your pathetic life." She pushed the pram outside and began to sprint down the long drive, finally taking her hands off the handle of the pram.

With baby Geoffrey asleep inside, the pram headed toward the gates of the property and the busy road outside the gates. Geoffrey woke up and began to cry, and Serge began to run after the pram. Kathleen stood watching in horror as her baby headed for the road, and Stephen, thinking the whole thing was a game, ran after his father and brother.

A few minutes earlier, Annette and George had parked on the road and were walking toward the gate, stopping to admire Serge's roses and herbs. Suddenly they saw the pram hurtling toward them, followed by Serge and Stephen. Annette screamed, and George threw himself at the pram to keep it from going onto the road. He stopped the pram, but Geoffrey fell out onto the concrete, bruising himself.

Annette was appalled and furious. "You are incompetent parents," she yelled at Serge and Kathleen. Then she turned to her son.

"I am surprised at you, Serge. You have no idea how to look after your newly born child. You never wanted him in the first place, and now you want to kill him," she said. "Geoffrey deserves better — he deserves a loving family."

Then she made a pronouncement that would change the course of Geoffrey's life: "As godparents to Geoffrey, we have an obligation to ensure he is looked after in proper hands. I am disgusted with you; this is not how we brought you up. We will not tolerate the treatment that Geoffrey is now enduring."

Turning to her husband, she said, "George, please take the pram. Geoffrey is coming with us."

Serge pleaded with her, explaining that the incident had been an accident, prompted by Kathleen's emotional outburst. He reminded his mother that Geoffrey was his and Kathleen's son, and he threatened to take her to court if she left with the child.

But Annette was unmoved. As far as she was concerned, Geoffrey was in grave danger in Serge's home. She did not think that Kathleen was a fit mother, and she did not think that Serge had control of his wife or his household. She had George put the baby in the car, and they started to drive off.

Serge ran desperately after the car, asking his parents to come back with his son. But George and Annette did not stop, and eventually the car began to move faster than Serge could run. Finally, he sank to the pavement, stunned and in tears.

CHAPTER TWO

Combining a Family

"Nobody can do for little children what grandparents do."

– Alex Haley

Geoffrey lived with Annette and George for the next five years. Serge continued to plead with his parents to return his son, and Kathleen continued to be furious that her in-laws had taken her son and that her husband seemed unable to get Geoffrey back.

Serge had tea with his mother every week, and he took the opportunity not only to see Geoffrey, but also to try to convince his parents that Geoffrey should live with him and Kathleen. Finally, five years after the day that George and Annette had taken Geoffrey home with them, they asked Serge to come for a meeting about the child's future.

Annette had her usual tea and cake ready when Serge arrived. He greeted his parents with respect and affection, and everyone felt the meeting was getting off to a positive start. Then George said, "Your mother and I have been thinking about the upbringing and well-being of young Geoffrey." He explained that he and Annette had been trying to provide Geoffrey with a loving environment and to instill in him the same values they had taught Serge when he was a boy. George explained that while they still loved Serge, they were concerned about returning Geoffrey to the care of Kathleen, whom they did not trust and whom they could not forgive for nearly pushing Geoffrey to his death in his pram. At the same time, George said, he and Annette realized that they were getting older and needed to find a way to bring Geoffrey's parents more fully into his life. However, he emphasized that he and Annette had no intention of giving up all control over Geoffrey's upbringing.

George said that he and Annette had decided that the best solution would be for them to sell their house and Serge and Kathleen to sell their house and for the two families to buy a house together. Geoffrey would continue to live with George and Annette in their part of the house, but Serge and Kathleen could see him whenever they wanted. Once George and Annette felt that Serge and Kathleen were ready to take over Geoffrey's care, they would revisit the arrangement.

Serge began to weep, and his mother came to his side to comfort him. "Serge, we love you and always wanted the best for you," she said gently. "You made choices, some of them against our better judgment, but we are trying to help, not alienate you from our love. But you are dealing with a little boy who needs love, support and a family."

She also reminded him about the day she and George took Geoffrey, saying, "If we had not arrived at the house when we did, Geoffrey might not even be with us today."

George said, "If you love your child, you will not only consider our suggestion but accept our proposal for the good of Geoffrey and the family. I feel we are being more than generous."

Serge realised that his parents were unlikely to let Geoffrey return to him and Kathleen and that this offer was his best chance to have full contact with his son. He also knew that the idea would infuriate Kathleen, who had expected Serge to insist that Geoffrey return to live with his parents and brother. But, having talked with George and Annette, Serge realized that the joint home idea was the only deal they were likely to approve, so he headed home to talk to Kathleen.

He drove around awhile to give himself more time to

consider ways to approach the discussion with Kathleen, but by the time he arrived home, he was so nervous that he could not get his key in the door. Kathleen, hearing the noise at the door, opened it. She knew from looking at Serge that the meeting had not gone as she hoped, and she immediately became angry, slamming the door in his face.

Serge was tired of being torn between his parents and his wife, and his main concern was to regain his son. So he came into the house and shouted, "Kathleen, stop. I have had enough of these arguments and your emotional games. I demand that we sit down now and discuss our son."

Kathleen was surprised by Serge's forcefulness, and she agreed to listen to what Serge had to say. But she was not pleased by the message he delivered. In fact, she was livid and told Serge that she would not live with his parents. She accused him of being weak, and she asked for a divorce. Serge remained strong and calm, though, pointing out that it was her behavior that had resulted in the loss of Geoffrey in the first place, and telling her that this was their best chance to get their son back.

He asked her bluntly, "Do you love Geoffrey, or is it that you cannot have Geoffrey?"

After several hours, Kathleen agreed to the plan, although she demanded that she have weekends away from the house and three holidays each year away from the children. Each family sold its home, and by about a year later they were living together in a large home in an address called "The Avenue." The house had 10 bedrooms, two lounges, a large kitchen, multiple living rooms and studies, and a large garden – which provided both families with plenty of space of their own.

However, there were still problems. There was a great deal of tension in the house, and Kathleen and her in-laws deeply disliked and distrusted each other, leaving Serge often in the middle. In addition, efforts to build Geoffrey's relationship with his brother faltered. Stephen was eight years older than Geoffrey and that age difference, coupled with the fact that Geoffrey had not lived with Stephen and his parents for years, resulted in Stephen not feeling particularly connected to his younger brother. Stephen also was becoming very attractive to girls, and at one point, he tried to impress his girlfriend by throwing Geoffrey down the stairs. Luckily for Geoffrey, Annette came home and put a stop to that activity.

After about five years in the single house, the families decided it would be best for everyone if they lived in separate houses. George and Annette agreed that Geoffrey could live with his parents and his brother, although they would continue to live nearby. Nine months later the joint house was sold, and the removal firm came to move the two families' belongings.

While everyone was finishing their packing, Kathleen confronted her younger son. He had become for her a kind of symbol of her misery. Because of him, she was embroiled in an ongoing power struggle with her in-laws. Because of him, she could not pursue a life of her own. Her anger at him boiled over, and she said, "You little bastard, listen here. You have ruined my life since you were born. I have been forced to endure a life of restriction because of you."

When Geoffrey tried to respond, she became enraged and began to hit him, first with her hand and then with a book. Finally, when he was black and blue, she threw him into a nearby wardrobe and locked the door. A few minutes later, when the removal team came and asked if they could take the wardrobe, Kathleen smiled and said, "Certainly. It's all yours."

Shortly after, Annette asked George if he had seen Geoffrey. The child could not be found, so the whole house and grounds were searched. Although Annette was frantic, the others decided that Geoffrey was playing hide-and-seek or otherwise being mischievous. Kathleen said nothing, and the moving company wanted to get their lorries under way.

The removal lorry left for George and Annette's new home, which was only 10 houses away from the home purchased by Kathleen and Serge; George and Annette had chosen a home so close so that they could keep an eye on Geoffrey.

A few hours later, the first lorry of Kathleen and Serge's furnishings was ready to go. When the removers arrived at the new place, they unloaded a few pieces and then came to the heavy wardrobe. As the removers were preparing to move the wardrobe, they heard a scream and knocking coming from the wardrobe. The wardrobe swayed and nearly fell over. The removers lifted the wardrobe to the ground and ran off to see if Serge had a key to the wardrobe.

Serge produced a key, and the wardrobe was opened to reveal young Geoffrey, who was shaking and crying and calling for his grandmother. Serge saw the bruises on his son, but the removal people assured him that the bruising could have happened while Geoffrey was locked in the wardrobe. Of course, there was still the question of how Geoffrey ended up locked in the wardrobe in the first place. Geoffrey would not offer an explanation and, although Annette and George were very suspicious that Kathleen had been responsible, Kathleen remained silent on the issue.

Life did not improve much for Geoffrey under the new arrangement of separate houses. Stephen went off to college, and Geoffrey tried to navigate the tensions in his household, often seeking refuge with his grandparents.

Kathleen, meanwhile, continued to be unhappy and dissatisfied with her life. Finally, she decided to look for a part-time job. She thought that getting outside her home and earning some extra money would make her life more fulfilling. One day while she was having her morning coffee, she saw an ad for a part-time job as an assistant to a small interior design business. The opportunity intrigued her, and she decided to follow up with the owner, who was named Hugo de Silva. De Silva asked her to come in for an interview.

Kathleen was nervous; she had been out of the workforce for decades, and she did not know how to act or what to wear. Without telling anyone in her family, she went to the interview, and she seemed to hit it off with de Silva. They chatted about a variety of topics, and finally he asked, "Do you really want this job?"

Kathleen responded, "Yes. You must understand that it is not just about the job, it's my independence — although the money will be useful, too."

De Silva liked Kathleen and was confident that she could do the job, but he was slightly concerned that her desire for the job reflected some problem in her life, and he was not sure he wanted to get involved in that. He told her he would take some time to think it over and would get back to her.

The waiting was tough on Kathleen, and therefore on

everyone else in the household. But after several days, de Silva called and offered her the job. She was to start the following Monday morning. Kathleen was overjoyed. She felt that the new job would give her independence and money of her own. She planned to announce her job at Sunday dinner.

Kathleen had never been much of a cook, so when her family saw her in the kitchen, they were surprised and a little confused. George and Annette had taken Geoffrey on an outing, and they arrived as Kathleen was preparing dinner. Annette realised that Kathleen was struggling in the kitchen, and she offered to help. Grudgingly, Kathleen accepted her help and invited Annette and George to stay for dinner.

Annette served a lovely dinner, and as the family began to eat, Kathleen thanked her mother-in-law for her help and then said that she had an announcement of her own. She said that since the move she had been unhappy and that she believed the unhappiness resulted from a lack of contact with other people. So, she explained, she had applied for a job, had been offered the position and would start work the next morning.

At first, everyone was stunned. Serge began to protest that she did not need to work and that she should continue to stay home with Geoffrey. George and Annette responded that they would be happy to watch Geoffrey while Kathleen worked, and that Serge and Kathleen probably could use the extra money for renovations they were doing to their property. Geoffrey was pleased to be left in the care of his grandparents, and Kathleen was surprised that her in-laws had supported her new job.

Shortly after she started, de Silva asked Kathleen to accompany him on a two-day weekend trip to London at which he would exhibit his business to clients and potential clients from London and from overseas. Kathleen accepted, although she did not tell Serge about the trip. On the day she left, she wrote a note to him telling him where she was going, and she left the note on his pillow.

De Silva arrived to pick her up driving a Rolls-Royce, and they were staying in the Savoy, one of London's most famous and elegant hotels. Everything about the trip enchanted Kathleen. She was fascinated by the hotel, the city and its people – and by her companion. While they were in London, Kathleen and de Silva slept together. Afterward, Kathleen felt terrible about what she had done. De Silva told her that his wife did not understand him, and he suggested that the affair could continue if Kathleen wanted it to. But Kathleen realized that she had been selfish and stupid to jeopardize her relationships with the people who loved her over a fling with a man she barely knew.

When she arrived home, she tried to deflect attention from her leaving so abruptly by being exceptionally cheerful and bringing gifts for everyone. Stephen and Geoffrey wanted to hear all about London, but finally Serge insisted on speaking with his wife. He was furious and accused her of having an affair, and their argument began to escalate. Soon they were yelling at each other. Young Geoffrey walked into the room as Kathleen threw a vase at Serge, and witnessing all the anger caused Geoffrey to vomit on the floor.

Finally, Serge and Kathleen took their fight behind closed doors. Serge insisted that Kathleen quit her job – which was a relief to Kathleen, although she would not admit it to Serge. She also never told him what had happened in London. They managed to patch things up, but the peace was only temporary.

CHAPTER THREE

On His Own

"In yourself right now is all the place you've got."

– Flannery O'Connor

By the time Geoffrey was 10, it was impossible to ignore the fact that his beloved grandparents, George and Annette, were aging. George in particular was experiencing health problems. He began having chest pain, and although he was treated by his doctor, he continued to suffer and to become weaker. Despite his difficulties, though, he maintained his cheerful disposition and his manners, always standing when the family – especially Annette – entered the room.

Walking became difficult for George, Often even on the short walk to Serge and Kathleen's house, he had to stop and take medication for his angina because the walk was uphill. But George enjoyed being outdoors, and he especially enjoyed the fact that when he got to Serge's house, he was always greeted warmly by his grandson.

George and Geoffrey shared a special bond, and they loved spending time together. Geoffrey always asked George about his trilby hat, saying "Grandfather, why do you always wear a hat? It is sunny today." George responded, "Young Geoffrey, you are right — the day is bright and very sunny. But it is also very windy, and the wind and cold temperature mean I need to wear my coat and my hat." He explained that heat from his body escaped through his head if he did not wear his hat. Geoffrey's questions often continued until George, amused, finally said, "You are a gift, my son. Come sit with me, and we will pay cards."

One day while George and Geoffrey were enjoying each

other's company, Serge was discussing with Annette his plans to add on a room, which he called the garden room, so that his family would have more space. Serge had an interest in architecture, and he enjoyed planning improvements to his home. However, he sometimes lacked the funds to complete the projects. He had asked the bank for a loan to cover this new room, but had been turned down. Now he asked his mother if she and George could give him some financial help.

At first, Annette was not happy with the request. She began to lecture Serge about his tendency to spend more than he should, and Serge became quiet and annoyed. Then Annette heard George cough softly, and she turned to him. A look passed between them that caused Annette to understand that her husband thought they should help out their son. Annette told Serge that she and George would lend Serge the money to add on the room. However, she said, they would consider it a loan, and he would have to make monthly payments.

Serge was thrilled with the offer, and readily accepted the terms. He started the project about a week later, enlisting the help of Geoffrey to dig trenches for the foundation. Soon, though, Kathleen began to get annoyed about the noise and the mess that the project was causing, and she and Serge were having a full-scale argument. To get away from the fighting, Geoffrey asked if he could go for a walk to collect conkers, or horse chestnuts. Serge thanked him for his help with the project and told him he could go, but he should be back by 5 p.m.

Geoffrey was very upset by the continuing arguments and unhappiness in his home. He washed up from his trench work and went to a secret hiding place in his bedroom where he kept his most precious possessions, including a small bag of coins that his grandfather had given him. Geoffrey took the bag and left the house, while his parents continued to battle.

Influenced by the time he had spent with his grandfather, Geoffrey enjoyed walking in the outdoors, especially in the spring and summer. His parents had put restrictions on where he was allowed to walk, and he headed down to Spilsbury Road, where there were a lot of conker trees. Geoffrey always had been fascinated by conkers and how the prickly green and brown casing could yield such a shiny nut. He loved to collect conkers, and he even had planted one once and watched the small tree grow, until his father ended that experiment.

Geoffrey used his time walking to think about things. He was very unhappy at home because of the difficult relationship of Serge and Kathleen. He compared them unfavourably to George and Annette, whom he considered his real parents. He arrived at Spilsbury Road and began to collect conkers. But soon he started to cry, eventually collapsing on the forest floor. He did not know what would become of him, and he thought about running away from home. Finally, he decided to take his bag of coins and head for the bus station to seek his fortune.

He had never been so far away from home on his own before, though, and soon he was lost. An older couple pointed him in the proper direction, but by the time he got to the station, it was 5:20. Serge was growing concerned about Geoffrey because it was unlike him to be late. He called George and Annette to see if Geoffrey had gone to visit them. George said the child was not with them, but he recognized from the tone of Serge's voice that something was wrong.

Serge told him that Geoffrey had gone out to collect conkers and was late getting back. George told Serge to stay at the house with Kathleen while George and Annette looked for him in the car. Before he left, though, George called the police.

Geoffrey had arrived at the bus station and found a pushing, shoving mob of people. Eventually he located a bus to London, and he asked the driver for a ticket. The next thing Geoffrey knew, he felt a hand on his shoulder and looked up to see a large policeman. The policeman asked Geoffrey where he was going and where his parents were.

Geoffrey responded, "I'm going to London, sir, and my parents are expecting me." But the officer knew Geoffrey was not telling the truth, so he took the child to the local police station. Since Geoffrey matched the description his grandfather had called in, the police called George, who said he would come and pick up Geoffrey.

George suggested to Geoffrey that he tell his parents he had lost track of time while looking for conkers. George was very upset that Geoffrey had been trying to run away, but he also realized that the child had a lot of problems at home and that telling his parents the whole story would only make those problems worse. George thought a better approach would be for him and Annette to spend more time with Geoffrey to try to determine what was bothering him so much that he wanted to run away. When they got back to Serge and Kathleen's home, George suggested that since the summer holidays were near, perhaps Geoffrey could spend some time with him and Annette. Over Kathleen's objections, Serge agreed.

That summer of 1977 was extremely hot in England, and Annette was worried about George. She knew that his health was deteriorating and that he was tired and often in pain, even though he did not admit to it. She and George decided to take Geoffrey with them to The New Forest, an area of southern England with a large expanse of heathland and woods. George and Annette had a cottage in The New Forest, and Annette thought that spending some time there with Geoffrey would be good for George.

The six weeks in The New Forest were rejuvenating for George. He always enjoyed being in nature, which was something he wanted to pass on to Geoffrey. And Geoffrey also enjoyed the time with his grandparents, spending time outdoors and going on adventures — which always ended with ice cream. For the first time in a long time, Geoffrey was able to relax, away from his tumultuous home life.

At the end of the holiday, Serge and Kathleen came to The New Forest. They stayed in a hotel rather than in the cottage, which worked better for everyone. The family decided to leave after the bank holiday in August so that Geoffrey could get ready for the next school term.

Shortly after returning home, George went out to cut the lawn. He used a push mower, which made the task particularly difficult. But George enjoyed working outdoors, and Annette always stopped him about midway through for a cup of tea and a biscuit. This time, though, as he was beginning to mow, he became short of breath and started to sweat. He had pain in his chest, and he collapsed. Annette, who was coming with the tea and biscuit, rushed to his side and found him lying there, shivering. She ran back in the house and called for an ambulance, which whisked George to the Royal Hampshire Hospital in Winchester.

When Annette got to the hospital, she called Serge, and he, Kathleen and Geoffrey joined her there. After some time, the doctors came out and told the family that George had had a severe heart attack and that they would have to monitor him to determine if there had been permanent damage.

George spent several weeks in hospital and, although he always managed a smile, he did not seem to be getting better and often even seemed weaker. One day he seemed particularly weak. When the family left from their visit, George seemed to take special care with his goodbyes, even telling Geoffrey to take care of his grandmother. Annette did not want to leave George's side because George was behaving so strangely, but finally she agreed to go home with Serge and Kathleen so that she would not have to stay alone.

Dinner was a pleasant distraction for Annette, who enjoyed having Stephen and especially Geoffrey around. But shortly after dinner, she retired to bed. It had been an emotional and exhausting day for everyone, and by 9 p.m. the whole household was in bed. At 3 a.m., everyone was awakened by the sound of the telephone. The hospital called to inform Annette that George had suffered a series of heart attacks and that, although he had fought valiantly and the hospital staff had done all they could, George had died; it was 9 November 1977. Both Annette and Geoffrey felt as if their whole world had been turned upside down, and they clung to each other and cried.

George was buried eight days later, and Serge – pushed by Kathleen – visited his mother a few days later. As usual, she invited him in and offered him tea and cake. Serge gladly accepted, but he was ill at ease, and Annette suspected why.

Finally, she said, "You are leaving me." Serge was surprised, but he admitted that she was correct – he and Kathleen had decided to move, taking Geoffrey and Stephen with them.

Annette was angry and sad. She told him that he was cruel to leave so soon after the death of his father, when she needed his help and support, and that she suspected that Kathleen was behind the decision. Serge had no response, and he left his mother broken-hearted and alone.

By June 1979, Kathleen and Serge had settled in a beautiful cottage in a country village called Bekesbourne, which was about 10 miles from Canterbury. Serge had a business opportunity in the area, but he also wanted to start his life over, away from his parents. Stephen was on his own, so Serge, Kathleen and Geoffrey formed a family life that was often fractious and uncomfortable, especially for Geoffrey, who missed his grandmother desperately.

Geoffrey found escape from his unhappiness by wandering the streets of Canterbury, soaking up the history and ideals of its famous residents like Sir Thomas Moore and Geoffrey Chaucer. He always had enjoyed learning, and he found many opportunities to expand his knowledge. But when he tried to share his thoughts with his parents, they were uninterested and dismissive. Only his grandmother seemed interested in hearing about what Geoffrey was doing and thinking. She loved hearing him talk about his studies and his interest in Canterbury, as well as his friends and his social activities. She seemed to sense that Geoffrey needed someone to listen to him, and she would always end their phone conversations by saying, "I am always here for you, only a telephone call away. I love you always."

Serge and Kathleen insisted that Geoffrey go to the local convent school, where they said he could learn discipline from the nuns, but he found school a welcome respite from his troubled home life. His neighbors, the Wests, had two sons, Stuart and Russell, who were actively involved with the Air Training Corps (ATC) Canterbury 312 Squadron. Soon Geoffrey enrolled as an Air Cadet. He also got a Saturday job at the shoe retailer Freeman Hardy and Willis, and between work, school and the ATC, Geoffrey was rarely home – which was just fine with him.

At home, Geoffrey always seemed to be in the way. Kathleen blamed him for everything that went wrong, even if Geoffrey was nowhere in the vicinity. He was often screamed at and even beaten. One Friday, he was coming home with Serge and carrying the fish that Serge had bought for dinner. Somehow the bag broke, and the fish fell to the ground. Kathleen began to yell that Geoffrey was at fault and that Serge should teach him a lesson so that he would not be so careless with expensive food. Serge, who realized that it has simply been an accident, tried to defend Geoffrey, but Kathleen would not listen. Finally, Serge took his son into the study and began to beat him with a belt. Geoffrey had suffered these beatings before, but for some reason he had had enough this time. He looked his father in the eye and said, "Is that the best you can give me father?" Serge beat him even harder, but Geoffrey just smiled. Finally, Serge called Kathleen, telling her than Geoffrey was too big for this treatment. In her rush to get to the study, Kathleen knocked over a vase that had been in her family for generations. She was furious at her husband and her son. She sent Geoffrey to his room, where he listened to the raised voices of his parents arguing. But neither of them ever struck him again.

Still, Geoffrey knew he could no longer endure the kind of home life he had. One November Sunday, he packed a small bag and went to the home of his friend David, who had said Geoffrey could stay at his house. David was a kind boy with loving parents, both of whom were pediatricians at the Kent and Canterbury Hospital. David's mother welcomed Geoffrey warmly, saying how glad she was that he had come to visit — she did not know he actually had run away from home. Geoffrey felt happier than he had since his grandfather's passing.

At the same time, Kathleen went to Geoffrey's room to get him for Mass. When she did not find him there, she told Serge that their son was missing. Serge thought he probably was with his ATC friends, and he went to ask Stuart and Russell West if they had seen him. When he did not find Geoffrey there, Serge returned and, ignoring Kathleen's accusation that his treatment of Geoffrey had caused the boy to run away, Serge called the police, the priest, the headmaster and some friends.

Luckily for Geoffrey, his parents did not have David's number. Geoffrey remained at David's house for several days, enjoying being in a peaceful household. He did not return to school, knowing that his parents would have alerted the school that he was missing, but David and he concealed from David's parents the fact that he was not going to school.

Finally, though, David's mother became suspicious. She

heard rumors at the school about a runaway boy, and she also noticed that Geoffrey never seemed to call and talk to his parents. At dinner that night, she said, "Geoffrey, do your parents miss you?" Geoffrey was slightly taken aback by the question. He replied that he was sure they did, but that he would be home soon. Later that evening, David's mother told Geoffrey that he must call his parents. She said that he had been with them for five days and, although they enjoyed having him, she suspected that there was a problem in his home.

Unhappily, Geoffrey called home. When Kathleen answered, he told her he would be home soon. When she began to berate him, he simply hung up. Then he packed his belongings, thanked David and his parents, and returned to the cottage. He said very little, but simply went to his room. A few minutes later, Serge knocked on Geoffrey's door and entered, saying, "Son, welcome home."

At school, he was given extra work so he could make up for the days he had missed. He began to study for his exams, which were coming in six months. He passed his exams in math, English, physics, biology, geography, art and domestic science, and his teachers wanted him to enter a sixth-year program to begin A levels. But Geoffrey was interested in college, and he enrolled in an electronics course at the local technical college.

In order to get away from his parents, Geoffrey continued to build a life of his own, often spending the night with friends after social events. When Geoffrey returned in the morning after one such night away from home, Kathleen met him at the door. She asked where he had been, and he explained that he had been out with friends and that since it was so late, he just stayed over. He told Kathleen he was planning to shower, and then they could all go to Mass.

Kathleen said, "It's simple, Geoffrey. If you want to stay out, you can leave." She threw his two suitcases down the stairs. Geoffrey picked up the suitcases and packed his belongings. Then he called a taxi and walked out the door — and into his own, independent life.

CHAPTER FOUR

Launching a Career

"Whatever you can do or dream you can do, begin it. Boldness has genius, power and magic in it."

– Goethe

After left his parents' house, Geoffrey moved in with a friend's brother and sister-in-law and started to look for a place of his own. Through another friend, he found a bedsit in a mansion property owned by a lady named Mrs. Donavera. Mrs. Donavera told Geoffrey that the rent was £30 a week, and electricity was extra. Geoffrey agreed, paid a month's rent in advance and moved in the following day. He was 16 years old, and he was completely on his own.

With rent to pay and the other expenses of living, Geoffrey needed an income. He found a job working three days a week and the occasional Sunday as a sales assistant at the Canterbury location of Rumbelows, a major U.K. electronics retailer. He also went to school, attending Canterbury Technical College. He earned £32.50 a week for working three days, and in addition he earned a commission that averaged £200 to £300 a month, so he had money for rent, food, education and even a social life.

He also had a big dream. After Geoffrey joined the Air Training Corp, he spent six weeks attending the Royal Air Force pre-entry school. There he learned about being in the RAF, flying helicopters and planes, and more. He was hooked; he desperately wanted to become a pilot. He loved hearing and seeing a Harrier Jump Jet on a flight run or exercise, and he dreamed of flying Mach 2 for the RAF. He sat for exams at the RAF recruitment office and was invited back for an interview. The next step was the pre-entry physical.

And that was where his RAF dream ended: He failed the

vision test. However, the people at the recruitment office had been so impressed with him that they offered him an engineering role. He asked if he could have a day or so to think about the offer, and they told him to take the time he needed. Geoffrey was devastated; he felt as if his whole world had been taken away from him. He went around for a while in a kind of a daze. But in the end, he decided that his dream had been to fly planes, not to fix them. He knew he had to move on and find his future in the civilian world.

He focused on his work with Rumbelows. Geoffrey was driven to succeed in his job, for a number of reasons. First, he needed the money. Unlike many other people his age, he was on his own, paying his own bills. If he wanted to keep a roof over his head and keep himself fed and clothed, he had to work. At the same time, he wanted to make a success of his life. He never wanted to have to go back to his family, and he wanted to show that he could support himself and even excel at his job.

He worked in the Rumbelows flagship store, which gave him access to additional resources such as training and an expansive product line. He grew into an excellent salesperson, consistently winning sales awards. In addition, he worked hard, volunteering whenever there was an opportunity for overtime. Soon he began to attract the attention of his superiors, who promoted him from part-time to full-time sales assistant to assistant manager of the store. He also was sent to trouble-shoot problems at other stores that were underperforming or to help with the launch of new stores. This experience taught him a great deal about what matters in business.

Geoffrey found that most of the underperformance was the result of poor attitudes on the part of the staff and an inability to engage with customers and to provide a good customer experience. Too often the salespeople were lazy or uninterested or even unpleasant. Either they did not know how to talk with customers, or they did not care. The experience taught Geoffrey the importance of good communication skills, both those of the sales staff with the customer and those of the company management with the sales staff.

His approach was extremely successful and drew the interest and enthusiastic support of management. In the last store he visited before moving on, for example, the store had been averaging £3,000 per week in sales. After Geoffrey had been at the store for a week, sales had increased to £7,000 per week; after four weeks, they were £14,500 per week. The store went from the worst-performing store in the area to the best-performing store, and from the bottom 10 per cent of stores in the country to one of the top 20 stores in the country.

Also around this time, Geoffrey joined a group of young business professionals. The group, which met once a month, was called the Business Institute of Management (BIM); it is now the Chartered Management Institute, or CMI. BIM was founded in 1947 as an organization to study and promote management best practices.

The Business Institute of Management gave even more definition to Geoffrey's life. He enjoyed learning about business and hearing from speakers such as Mark H. McCormack, author of a number of best-selling books including "What They Don't Teach You at Harvard Business

School." The author became an inspiration to Geoffrey. McCormack, who died in 2003, was a lawyer and a golfer who became a sports agent and later the founder of International Management Group, now IMG, which serves the sports, entertainment, fashion and media industries. His first client was Arnold Palmer, an American golfer who won a total of seven major tournaments, including The Masters in 1958, 1960, 1962 and 1964; the U.S. Open in 1960; and The Open Championship, now the British Open, in 1961 and 1962. In addition to Palmer, McCormack's company also represented golfers Gary Player and Jack Nicklaus. He expanded his client roster to include many famous tennis players and other athletes, as well as models and people from the entertainment industry. Geoffrey was fascinated by McCormack's ability to create a highly successful business by following his passion.

The Business Institute of Management also introduced Geoffrey to many people who, he realized, were much like himself. He could talk to them about business issues and opportunities, and he began to understand that there were no limits to what he could accomplish if he were willing to work hard and to learn. The experience helped to draw him further from the traumatic world of his childhood and into a world in which he was responsible for his own future.

One of his friends at the Institute, Brian O'Connell, was a university professor. He took an interest in Geoffrey and tried to persuade Geoffrey to sit for an MBA degree. Geoffrey did not study for an MBA with O'Connell, although years later, in 2004, he did get an MBA in Business Administration from Trinity University in San Antonio, Texas. But O'Connell introduced Geoffrey to someone who would be responsible for launching Geoffrey into his career: the Managing Director of Commercial Business Operations for a large American bank.

The man was impressed by Geoffrey, and he invited Geoffrey to visit the bank. In turn, Geoffrey was intrigued by the bank – it was a large American enterprise and had reach far exceeding that of any company Geoffrey had ever known.

Geoffrey was only 20, but his abilities and his work ethic impressed his contact so much that the older man told him that the bank was looking for someone with vision and drive to market a new financial product to insurance companies. That person would have extensive freedom to design and execute a strategy with national and regional support from the bank. He asked Geoffrey to think about the opportunity.

Geoffrey was very interested. He knew that he had shown the ability to motivate people and to market successfully at Rumbelows, and he was intrigued by the opportunity to put his talents to work on a much larger scale. He realized that marketing on behalf of a major international bank was much more challenging than selling electronics in a retail store, but he believed he was up to the challenge.

At the bank, Geoffrey met with the head of Marketing, the head of Commercial Finance, the head of Operations, and Human Resources. A short time later, he was offered a job. He asked if he could have some time to evaluate the offer, which he then discussed with Brian O'Connell, his professor friend from the Business Institute of Management who had introduced him to the Managing Director. After consulting with O'Connell and considering his options, Geoffrey accepted the position as Development Officer for the financial product.

41

The Managing Director smiled at the news and said, "Geoffrey, we have every faith in your abilities. The only caveat is that if you fail, you will be fired." Geoffrey left the man's office with the realisation that he was about to begin his first real job, to take a step into the unknown and test himself and his abilities in the real world of international business. He was proud, and excited to begin the test.

Once he started his new job, Geoffrey discovered that he had a lot to learn. He studied operations manuals, took training course after training course, and sat for exam after exam; his final exam was the commercial underwriters exam. Once he finished his training and education, he was tasked with the strategy of building the U.K. network, marketing and administration plan for his product, which provided commercial loans. The strategy was to work with commercial underwriters to reach their large business clients, using the insurance companies as a distribution mechanism. Under Geoffrey's guidance, the large American bank in the U.K. reached agreements with major UK. insurers.

Once the rollout of the product began, it was up to Geoffrey to identify, recruit and train new development managers around the United Kingdom. His goal was to find other people who, like himself, had exceptional people skills and business instincts and who were willing to work very hard. That approach worked, and the product became a major success for the bank — and for Geoffrey.

The success of the product rollout would have been impressive under any circumstances, but it was especially so because Geoffrey was so young — only 20 when he started at the bank. At an age when many young men were just finishing up at university and starting in an entry-level job, Geoffrey had his degree and had landed a position of responsibility in a major multinational company.

To some extent, though, Geoffrey always had been a kind of old soul. He was raised in large part by his grandparents, and his parents were at best distant and at worst emotionally and physically abusive. He was, for all intents and purposes, an only child; his brother was eight years older, and they were not close. So he was often alone, left to entertain himself on his own and highly motivated to avoid attracting the attention of his parents, especially his mother.

He also was determined to succeed. In a very real sense, he had no option. He had been asked to leave his parents' house – and he had been more than happy to go. But he was on his own, responsible for his own success or failure. And his grandparents had taught him some values that served him well as he built his career.

The first was to work hard. Geoffrey was usually the first person into the office and the last person out. He was willing to do whatever was necessary to achieve his goals. He was enthusiastic and threw himself wholeheartedly into whatever challenge presented itself. He delivered things ahead of deadline, and he was always available to discuss the status of his projects.

He also was eager to learn and a quick study. His grandparents had helped him develop his innate curiosity about the world around him, and he translated that to his work. He was very interested in understanding how the company operated. While many of his peers were content with a kind of passivity, waiting for management to decide what they should do, Geoffrey was determined to engage with management. He asked questions, and he offered suggestions. That impressed his superiors, who usually were more than happy to talk about their job and their philosophy with an eager young man who was clearly going places.

Geoffrey knew that he had been handed an exceptional opportunity with the bank job, and he was determined to make the most of it. He soaked up all the knowledge he could about the banking system and about banking and business processes. He was excited to be working in the real world of high finance and, while he was occasionally nervous, he never felt that he was overmatched or underprepared.

He began to learn how to take advantage of the huge amounts of data available in a company like the bank. He became convinced that, with access to sufficient data and information, even a relative newcomer like himself could design and execute a successful strategy. The key was to rely on the data in developing and then in continually evaluating the plan.

He also became even more convinced that there are certain constants in business success, no matter what the business. Both as a sales assistant at Rumbelows and as a development officer at the bank, there were several qualities that Geoffrey drew on to achieve his goals. First, he believed it was important to be engaged in your work. When he went to Rumbelows stores to determine why sales were not good, he often found that the salespeople simply did not seem to care. They were not enthusiastic, and they did not interact with customers in a meaningful way. He realized that the person leading a business effort – whether that effort involves selling electronics or launching a financial product – needs to actually lead; he can't simply sit by and wait for things to happen.

He also learned the importance of always going the extra mile. In order to achieve more than the next person, it is necessary to be willing to do more. Sometimes that means putting in extra hours or extra effort in some other way, but that can pay off in the long run.

And he realized it is important to be willing to take a risk. As he rose through the ranks at Rumbelows and then at the bank, he often accepted responsibilities that many might have thought he was too young or not sufficiently qualified to take on. But Geoffrey believed in himself, and he knew that he was capable of accomplishing what he set out to do.

Eventually, though, Geoffrey was ready for something new. The first training manual that he received at the bank showed a picture of the firm's global headquarters in New York, and he made it a goal to one day work there or to work in management at one of the bank's subsidiaries or affiliate companies.

Geoffrey was fascinated by the United States, and that fascination was only fueled by working for a U.S.-based company. He admired the optimism of America, which he felt sometimes contrasted with a stoic or even pessimistic approach in Europe. It seemed that Americans believed that anything was possible, that they could accomplish whatever they set out to do – which was a belief that Geoffrey shared. In addition, he felt that the United States was a much bigger player in the business world than was the United Kingdom, and that it offered much greater opportunities for an ambitious and talented young man.

However, every time Geoffrey applied for a new position within the bank, either the position was no longer available or he seemed blocked in his efforts to move up the company ladder. He became increasingly frustrated by what he saw as management's unwillingness to allow him to advance and take on greater responsibilities in the organization.

Finally Geoffrey realized that, although he was grateful to have been given his first real business opportunity, he was ready to move on. He had been with the company for five years, and he wanted some new challenges. He resigned and, although management tried to talk him out of leaving, he was ready to take the next step in his career.

CHAPTER FIVE

A Lesson in Love

"Keep love in your heart. A life without it is like a sunless garden when the flowers are dead."

– Oscar Wilde

After leaving the bank in 1992, Geoffrey approached a design company that specialized in museums, conferences and exhibitions, which was a far way from banking. But Geoffrey was anxious for the opportunity to work internationally across marketing programs. He was hired as the company's European Marketing Manager, and he designed, created and executed marketing programs in a variety of industries ranging from banks to telecom to automotive and aerospace programs across Europe and North America.

His professional life was on track, but Geoffrey knew there was something missing in his personal life. Although he had had several girlfriends, he had not found someone to whom he could commit himself. And he realized that part of the problem might be him. His life with his parents had been volatile and confusing, and Serge and Kathleen had not presented him with anything remotely resembling an example of a healthy marriage. In the chaos of their house, he had been often alone, dependent on only himself. He realized that his childhood had helped to make him untrusting and unwilling to hand his heart fully to another.

On the other hand, his grandparents, George and Annette, had shown him an excellent example of a loving relationship. They had loved each other, and they had loved him unconditionally. They had created a safe place for him amid the tumult of his parents' home, and they continually had impressed on him the importance of the values they practiced every day.

Geoffrey desperately wanted to find the kind of happiness that his grandparents had. He wanted to find a woman to whom he could commit himself completely, body and soul, and with whom he could create a life into which they would grow old together.

George and Annette wanted that for Geoffrey, too. As he became an adult, after his grandfather had died, Annette often spoke to him of her hopes. "Grandson, I want you to be happy before I go," she would say. "You deserve happiness and a life in love, true love."

Geoffrey would jokingly reply that he had no time for love, that starting and growing his career took all his time and attention. But Annette was persistent. One day in 1996, when Geoffrey had been with the design group for four years and had established himself there, Annette brought it up again.

"One of the most important things in life is love, waking up in the morning knowing you have love infinitely," she said. "Geoffrey, you are a wonderful person. Your grandfather and I always considered you a gift in our life, and you will find someone in your life who feels the same way. You deserve to be happy, and it would make me happy to know that you were in love and happy."

For some reason, Geoffrey did not give her his usual glib response about being too busy to look for love. Instead, he said, "I am going on holiday next week, Grandmother. It's time to have a break. I am quite exhausted from work. But while I am on holiday, I will think about what you said." Annette smiled and began her ritual of serving tea and cake.

Geoffrey had booked a holiday to Jamaica. He had been invited to stay with friends in San Marco Island, Florida, but at the last minute he decided he needed some time by himself. He headed for a resort, determined to sit on the beach in the sunshine, read and re-energize without the distractions of work.

The flight to Montego Bay was pleasant, and Geoffrey quickly passed through customs and collected his luggage. When he walked outside, he saw a driver carrying a sign that said, "Mr. Geoffrey." Geoffrey walked up to the driver and nodded, and the driver introduced himself as Zachary. He loaded Geoffrey's luggage into a silver Mercedes, and they headed for the resort. Geoffrey found himself beginning to relax in the warm island sunshine.

The resort was a gated property and had gorgeous gardens with lush greenery and waterfalls. At check-in, Geoffrey was upgraded to a beach cottage. The resort had 10 cottages, each facing the ocean and very private. Geoffrey began to unpack and settle in. He put a CD in the stereo system and decided to treat himself to a relaxing bath and an early dinner before jet lag set in.

After his bath, Geoffrey dressed and headed for the bar. He asked the bartender, whose name was Lewis, what he would suggest. Lewis went through the options and, as Geoffrey was ordering a Sex on the Beach cocktail, he realized that he had attracted the attention of a stunning young lady who appeared to be on her own. She smiled at him, and he held her gaze.

Just as it was becoming uncomfortable, Lewis returned with Geoffrey's drink. As Geoffrey was signing the bill, Lewis said, "I am minding my own business, but there seems to be some intense energy between you and the beauty over there."

When Geoffrey did not respond, Lewis continued, "Just to let you know, she has been in the hotel the last few days. Many guys have approached her, but she has stayed away. But there certainly does seem to be some chemistry for you, my man." Geoffrey smiled and said nothing, but he gave Lewis a large tip.

Then he settled back with his drink to watch the sunset – and to steal another glance at the beautiful woman. He had not spoken to her and he did not know her name, but Geoffrey could not help but feel that the two of them had made a connection.

The next morning Geoffrey decided to take a walk on the beach at sunrise. He wanted to brush away the cobwebs, take a deep breath of fresh sea air and watch the waves crash against his feet as he walked. He came to a small beach café, where he stopped for breakfast before continuing his stroll. As he ate, he could not help but think back to the woman from the night before. Even after a good night's sleep, he could not shake the feeling that they had made a connection. When he finished breakfast, he continued his walk.

There were very few people on the beach so early in the morning, which made it perfect for walking and thinking. Then, in the distance, Geoffrey saw someone who seemed remarkably familiar. As the figure approached, he realized it was the young lady he had seen in the bar. She was walking along the beach in a bikini and listening to music. They stopped and looked at each other, and finally Geoffrey introduced himself.

In an accent that was partly American and partly Latin, the young lady responded, "It is a pleasure to meet you. My name is Marcela."

They began to talk, and they soon found that the conversation was very easy. They talked about the arts, poetry, culture and their lives in their home countries. Marcela had been educated at Oxford University in England, and she had a law degree from Georgetown University in Washington, D.C. She was an environmental lawyer in her home town of San Jose, Costa Rica.

They talked all day, never running out of things to discuss. Then as the sun began to sink into the ocean, they started to walk back to the resort. Marcela reached for Geoffrey's hand, and as she did, he turned and kissed her.

Geoffrey was stunned by what was happening. He no longer felt alone; he felt complete with Marcela. He could not believe that he had heard his grandmother's wish for him right before he left for Jamaica, and now he had found a woman he thought he might be able to love for the rest of his life. He knew it was crazy, but he also knew how he felt. He whispered to Marcela, "I love you." And she responded, "I know. That is exactly how I feel."

When they got back to the resort, they stopped at the bar for a drink. Lewis the bartender could not help but smile when he saw them. "Ya, man, so are we serving champagne for the lady and yourself?" he asked Geoffrey. Geoffrey smiled and said to bring the champagne in an ice bucket. When they were finished with the champagne, they retired to Geoffrey's cottage.

Marcela was due to fly back to Costa Rica on the following Friday, but neither she nor Geoffrey wanted to think about her departure. They decided to go to a local restaurant for a romantic dinner the night before she was scheduled to leave.

The restaurant was on the beach and was built on stilts overlooking the water. They dressed up for their dinner and arranged for a car to take them to the restaurant.

They both picked at their food, trying to avoid thinking about their coming separation. When dinner was over, Marcela suggested that they walk back to the resort. It was a beautiful night, and she wanted to enjoy the sand, the water, the stars and the full moon. They took off their shoes and chased each other through the edge of the surf. Geoffrey looked into Marcela's eyes, and he felt his heart crumble.

There were many tears when it came time for Marcela to leave for the airport, but the two promised to find ways to be together again. Geoffrey kept busy with horseback riding, snorkeling and excursions around the island until it was his turn to go home.

On the flight back to London, Geoffrey reflected on his relationship with Marcela. He realized that he had known her only a few days and that they came from very different worlds. But he had never had such an intense connection with anyone, and he knew that he wanted to see her again.

When he returned to the U.K., he called Marcela and told her that he thought they must find a way to continue their relationship. She agreed, saying that she too had never felt this way about someone. They determined that Marcela could meet Geoffrey in Miami when he traveled to the United States, which was often. The pair met every four to six weeks for three years, and they continued to delight in each other's company.

Finally, though, Marcela's parents thought that it was about time that they met their daughter's love. Her father was an important businessman who controlled several coffee and banana plantations in Costa Rica. He was very protective of his family, and he thought that, since he had been paying for Marcela's travel expenses to Miami, it was time for Geoffrey to come and make his intentions clear. Marcela asked Geoffrey to come to San Jose to meet her family, explaining that she felt it was time to take this next step in their relationship.

Geoffrey was extremely busy at work, especially because of the time he took out of his schedule to meet Marcela in Miami. But he loved her deeply, so when she asked him to come to Costa Rica, he agreed and booked a flight.

When Marcela picked Geoffrey up at the airport, she looked especially lovely. She drove him to the hotel where he was to stay at the beginning of his visit, and he showered and changed clothes. Then they went to Marcela's home to meet her family.

Marcela's family lived in a large gated home with a huge courtyard. When they arrived, Geoffrey was greeted by Marcela's mother, Monita. Monita was a charming woman and an excellent conversationalist; she and Geoffrey talked about a variety of topics. She spoke excellent English, and Geoffrey even added a few thoughts in Spanish, which she appreciated.

On the other hand, Marcela's father, Santiago, seemed distant and almost unfriendly. Monita managed to keep the conversation interesting and upbeat through the afternoon and during dinner, but Geoffrey got the feeling that Santiago was uncomfortable around Geoffrey and that the older man had something specific on his mind.

After dinner, Marcela told her parents that Geoffrey was

tired from his travels and that she was going to drive him back to his hotel. Monita was charming as always, but Santiago seemed happy to see him go. On the drive back to the hotel, Geoffrey told Marcela his observations about her father, wondering aloud what the problem was.

Marcela dismissed his concerns, saying, "Geoffrey my dear, I am his little girl, and he is a Costa Rican man. If you were in his position, you probably would feel the same way. Mama adores you, which is the important thing. And I love you, so be happy."

Geoffrey apologized, explaining that jet lag probably was to blame for his disgruntled mood. Marcela laughed off his apology and suggested that he get a good night's sleep. She told him she had to work in the morning but that she would come to his hotel in the afternoon so they could spend time alone together before going back to her home.

When Marcela arrived the next afternoon, she told Geoffrey she wanted to talk to him about something. When Geoffrey asked what that was, Marcela said, "I found out why my father was a little hostile with you yesterday. My father believes that you should make an honest woman of me. His offer is that you should marry me in San Jose and he will provide a house for us to live in near the family and provide you with a good salary and a role as an executive in his company."

Geoffrey was stunned. It was not that he did not want to be with Marcela. In fact, he told her, "To marry you would be an honor." But he noted that to accept her father's offer would mean that he would have to leave his country and the career he was working so hard to build.

Marcela replied, "This is a very respectable offer by my father and one that would make him happy about us and importantly about you. But we have plenty of time to discuss the details."

For the next few days, Geoffrey and Marcela visited many places in Costa Rica. Marcela showed him the beauty of her country and reminded him of how much they loved each other. But Geoffrey was very conflicted about the plan. He had spent several years building a successful business career in London. He liked his work, he was good at it, and he was well-respected. He was not at all sure he wanted to give that up to move to Costa Rica and work for his father-in-law.

In addition, the U.K. was home. It was his country, and he was comfortable and familiar with it. He had friends there. And there was also his grandmother, whose health was beginning to fail. He knew that, although she would want him to be happy even if it meant moving, he could never forgive himself if he were 7,000 miles away when she needed him.

Gradually he came to the realization that he could not accept Santiago's offer and stay in Costa Rica, even if it meant he would lose Marcela. On his last day, he told Marcela that he would take the hotel courtesy bus to the airport the next day. She objected, saying that she always saw him off and that, even though it was hard to say goodbye, she wanted to take him to the airport.

When Marcela drove Geoffrey to the airport the next day, neither of them spoke. Finally, Marcela began to cry as she realized that Geoffrey had made his decision and that the decision was to leave her. She looked at him and said, "This is it – am I right?"

He could only look at her, but his answer was clear in his silence. By the time they arrived at the airport, they were both in tears. Marcela begged him to reconsider and to stay with her in Costa Rica, but Geoffrey knew he could not. He kissed her a final time and walked into the airport.

This was the most difficult decision Geoffrey had ever had to make. Although he believed he had made the right choice, he also knew that it was possible that he would never see Marcela again – and that he would never again meet a woman he loved as much.

When he returned to London, he threw himself into his work. He focused even harder on his career, and he found himself traveling even more. He achieved some of his greatest successes, but he always felt there was something missing.

About three years after he left Costa Rica, he met a woman named Caroline at work. She was the opposite of Marcela – English and very supportive of his career and his travel. The relationship began as colleagues, but over time it progressed, and eventually Geoffrey and Caroline were married.

CHAPTER SIX

A Lesson in Loss

"Mostly it is loss which teaches us about the worth of things."

– Arthur Schopenhauer

After being with the design company for about four years, a headhunter approached Geoffrey about working for another design company. This company was similar to the previous company, but this was a boutique company. Its growth had reached a plateau, and the company was looking for someone to re-energize it and help it grow to a larger, more profitable firm. The challenge appealed to Geoffrey, and he signed on as a Business Development Director in 1997.

Geoffrey helped the company to accomplish a remarkable turnaround, and within a short time, Compaq Computer Corporation asked the company to bid on the launch of Compaq's first-ever foray into telecommunications. Geoffrey already was working with Digital Equipment Corporation when he received a brief for the Compaq launch. Geoffrey's company was pitching against some of the biggest agencies in the world, and some people within the company felt that it was not ready for a job of this magnitude.

However, Geoffrey believed it was time to push the boundaries of the company. It was a huge opportunity, and it would put the company on the map. They got the job, and the firm made the launch a success. The goal was to create a worldwide identity for Compaq in telecommunications, and Geoffrey and his team met that goal. The project morphed into an integrated worldwide design strategy, which resulted in many other projects and a big influx of cash for the company. Soon after the Compaq success, Infogrames commissioned the company to handle its launch into the United States. Soon the company was involved in a variety of new industries, including telecom, interactive gaming, automotive, aerospace, and oil and gas, and it was working internationally, not only in Europe but also in Africa, the Middle East, North America, Asia and the Pacific.

Geoffrey's work life now had taken him from banking to marketing programs, and through his experience with the Compaq launch, he had gained enormous international experience. He was running global marketing and rollout efforts that required him to adapt to different cultures and performance measures. He was stretching himself to work far more strategically.

He also was traveling more or less nonstop, making up to 60 international trips a year. In September 2001, he headed for New York on the first leg of a trip that was also to take him to Houston, Austin, Los Angeles, Atlanta and Washington, D.C. before his return to London.

On his previous trips to New York, Geoffrey always had stayed in the Marriott hotel at the World Trade Center because the location was convenient to meeting clients. But because of an unsatisfactory experience at a different Marriott property, he decided to take the advice of a colleague and stay at the Hyatt in midtown.

That decision could have saved his life. On the morning of September 11, terrorists flew airplanes into the twin towers, ultimately collapsing the buildings and killing more than 2,500 people. Hundreds more died in coordinated attacks on the Pentagon in Washington and when passengers forced the crash of a plane in Pennsylvania that had been hijacked by terrorists.

These were the first attacks on American soil since the Japanese attack on Pearl Harbor in 1941, and they rattled the country – and much of the world – to its very core.

Geoffrey watched the firemen hose down the grey dust on the crumpled towers, and when he looked into the eyes of those firemen, he glimpsed the depth of their sadness but also the power of their resolve to survive and rise above this attack. It was an image that would stay with him forever.

Once air travel returned to normal after the attacks, Geoffrey resumed his travels, although he skipped his visit to Washington. When he finally arrived back in London, his colleagues applauded as he walked into the office. He was grateful for their support, and he was very glad to be home.

By 2002, Geoffrey was suffering as a result of the breakdown of his relationship with Caroline. There were many problems in his marriage, including his inability to forget Marcela. Finally, Geoffrey and Caroline decided to divorce and sold their house. Geoffrey moved into another house not far from the house they had shared, and he was once again on his own.

At the same time, Annette was becoming increasingly frail, and Geoffrey was growing increasingly worried about her. He visited her over the 2003 August bank holiday, bringing her flowers and a cake and, as usual, she showered him with her love. They reminisced and talked about the future, conversations that left Geoffrey feeling happy despite his sadness over his divorce.

On the Monday of the bank holiday, Geoffrey's parents, Serge and Kathleen, visited Annette. It was Kathleen's birthday, and Annette was in a particularly happy mood following Geoffrey's visit. She invited her son and daughter-in-law in for tea and cake. The big bouquet of fresh flowers made it obvious that Geoffrey had visited recently, and Kathleen was not pleased.

"You have seen Geoffrey," she said in an accusatory way to her mother-in-law.

Annette never thought that Kathleen deserved Geoffrey, and she was proud that he continued to come to visit her. She said, "That's right. He came to see me yesterday. He has been traveling, you know."

Serge asked if his son were well, and Annette replied that he was very well. She said that he had finalized the divorce with Caroline. She added that the divorce and all the travel were hard on him, but that he knew his grandmother loved him.

That comment infuriated Kathleen, who said, "He is our son – how dare you say that!"

Annette's anger boiled over. She stood up and told Kathleen that Kathleen had never been a proper mother to Geoffrey and that she, Annette, had been both mother and grandmother. She said that it was through the efforts of herself and George and not Kathleen and Serge that Geoffrey had grown into a fine and successful man, and that it was a shame that Kathleen's behavior had kept her from being a part of Geoffrey's life.

Kathleen jumped to her feet to confront her mother-in-law, and she accidentally knocked Annette to the floor. Serge tried to act as peacemaker, but when he realized that his mother had fainted, he called for an ambulance, which took Annette to hospital.

Annette was quite elderly, and she had been suffering from a variety of ailments including angina, diabetes, sciatica and more. She had been undergoing several medical tests and taking more than 38 tablets a day – a regimen that she despised.

Geoffrey received a phone call from his brother, Stephen; since Geoffrey was estranged from his parents, it was always Stephen who communicated family news. Stephen told Geoffrey what had happened and urged him to go to the hospital immediately. Geoffrey was stunned, especially since he had just seen his grandmother and she had seemed to be in good health at the time.

Geoffrey visited Annette in hospital every other day, bringing her flowers, tea and cake and reassuring her that she would soon be able to go home. Annette was in The Royal Hampshire Hospital, the same hospital where her husband, George, had died years earlier. Geoffrey was constantly aware of the loss he had already suffered there, and he did not want to lose his beloved grandmother as well.

After Annette had been in hospital for several weeks, Geoffrey told her that he had received a job offer from a company in America to run its operations in Europe, the Middle East and Africa (EMEA). The company had been failing financially for several years and wanted to make some changes. Geoffrey was intrigued, though he knew that taking the position would bring many challenges and take lots of time and hard work.

He told his grandmother about the offer, and he said that the CEO wanted to see him in New York the following week if he decided to take the job. He did not want to leave his grandmother, but she told him that he should go. She reminded him of how proud she was of all that he had accomplished, and she added that she did not want him to jeopardize or slow down his career on her account.

He told her he worried because the job would involve a lot of traveling, which would mean he would not be able to spend as much time with her. But she smiled and responded, "You need to go my son. I will be fine. This is your life, so go and make this a success. I love you – never forget this. And I am always going to be with you."

Geoffrey flew to New York to accept the job and to meet with his new chief executive officer and the executive team, and then he flew back to England to see his grandmother. He had a quiet week and was able to visit Annette every day in hospital. He had an early flight to Milan on Saturday morning, but when he left Annette on Friday he promised to visit her on Monday after he returned.

When Geoffrey got home after his trip, he saw that his brother, Stephen, had called and left a message. In the message, Stephen apologized for misplacing Geoffrey's mobile number and told Geoffrey that Annette had passed away around 4 a.m. on Saturday, November 8. Geoffrey was devastated. He called Stephen to find out more about what had happened and, when he hung up with Stephen, he went to his wine cellar and got several vintage bottles of Italian red wine.

There were two people who had always told Geoffrey that he could call them when his grandmother died, no matter what the time or situation. The first was his ex-wife, Caroline. He called her and, although she was polite, it was very clear that she had company and was not really interested in talking to Geoffrey. He then called an old friend named Andrew, and he got the same kind of polite but ultimately disinterested response. He was left alone with his sadness.

After another bottle of wine, he decided to call an American friend named Robert, who was an executive with Compaq Computer Corporation. He told Robert what had happened, and Robert was immediately sympathetic and wanted to know what he could do to help. Geoffrey told Robert that he had a trip planned to the United States, including Las Vegas, and Robert offered to join Geoffrey in Las Vegas so they could spend some time together and he could help Geoffrey work through his grief. Geoffrey was very grateful for Robert's friendship and for the opportunity to talk about his grandmother with a good friend.

To help deal with the loss of his grandmother, Geoffrey also threw himself into his work. And there was a lot of work that needed to be done at his new firm, which was a technology company that manufactured a digital display product used in outdoor advertising. He started with a visit to the company's offices and production facilities in the United States, including Las Vegas. He then completed a SWOT (Strengths, Weaknesses, Opportunities and Threats) analysis across 12 countries. He developed recommendations for making changes and improvements, and he presented this report – and the budget needed to implement it – at the New York office.

Among his recommendations were to relocate the European headquarters to the United Kingdom from the Netherlands; to consolidate some offices to increase efficiency and reduce costs; to improve collections, customer service, manufacturing and operations, and sales and marketing; and to relaunch the EMEA operation with new and improved product offerings, new Key Performance Indicators (KPIs) and new staffing and budgeting – and to accomplish all this within 12 weeks.

Geoffrey met his own deadline, and his new approach paid off. Over a period of six to nine months, the company increased profitability and performance in the EMEA operation, which had once been a money loser. In addition to finding ways to cut costs and improve productivity, Geoffrey uncovered corruption in the company that led to the firing of several people and then the rebuilding of the staff. He also changed the sales approach from a product bias to a solution bias. In other words, instead of focusing on selling a single product, the focus changed to creating solutions for customers, which encouraged up-selling and cross-selling. This had an immediate and very positive effect on sales, and it resulted in a much better performance overall for the EMEA region. The job also involved a great deal of traveling: He made 90 international trips in about 12 months from 2003 to 2004.

Management was pleased and impressed by the work that Geoffrey had done for them. Geoffrey wanted to create and lead a global communications effort, and he approached the CEO about the possibility of leading the company's global marketing and communications. However, this was not the future the CEO saw for Geoffrey.

At about the same time, Geoffrey was approached by a headhunter in London who specialized in recruitment for telecom and IT marketing. The headhunter took Geoffrey to lunch, where he complimented Geoffrey effusively about his work at his current employer and then told Geoffrey that a client would like to meet with him to discuss an opportunity in which he would manage a group of about 60 people. However, the headhunter said, the company was based in Moscow, so the person who took this job would have to move there.

Geoffrey thought for a few minutes, and then he said that he would be interested in exploring the opportunity further and in having a discussion with the client. At this point he did not know anything about the company other than it was based in Moscow.

Geoffrey ultimately had six interviews, including meetings with the head of Human Resources, the CEO, the management team and consultants in New York and finally in Moscow. Geoffrey accepted the job and headed to Moscow, where the company had arranged for his relocation, including finding him an apartment and handling the necessary paperwork.

Geoffrey found that the company was unorganized by western standards and that it had no real strategy for communications. He reorganized his department to function as an integrated team, and he devised and implemented a marketing strategy for the company in the United States and Europe.

However, politics soon interceded. In September 2004, Chechen extremists took over a school in Beslan, Russia. They held more than 1,000 students hostage in a siege that lasted two days and ended in the deaths of more than 330 civilians. At around the same time, the train station near where Geoffrey lived was blown up, and two passenger planes exploded in coordinated bombings, killing 90 people. Geoffrey decided it was no longer safe for him to stay in Russia, and by December 2004 he was back on British soil, and looking for work again.

CHAPTER SEVEN

The Start of a Dream

"*Remember that wherever your heart is, there you will find your treasure. You've got to find the treasure, so that everything you have learned along the way can make sense.*"

– Paulo Coelho

When Geoffrey returned from Russia, he was ready for a change. He realized that he had amassed a wide range of knowledge and experience throughout his career. In fact, in 2002 he had set up an entity called PMI Consulting Limited, although he never had actually operated under the company banner. However, when he returned from Russia, he thought the time was right to strike out on his own.

Basically, PMI consisted of Geoffrey – he was a one-man shop, working with some of his international clients on a combination of strategic consulting, brand strategy and marketing programs. He had some major successes, including a brand and marketing review that helped the Finland-based Wartsila Group set up a successful sales operation in China, a rebrand of a U.K. government agency into what is now TechUK, and marketing programs for Ford of Europe, Compaq Computer Corporation and CLS Bank. But by 2005, he had begun to realize that his business model for PMI was flawed.

First, it relied too heavily on him. That meant that he was limited as to what he could do, which obviously restricted his ability to grow the business. And it also meant that he was operating without the input, feedback and support of a team. He knew that he would need to make adjustments if PMI were to be a long-term proposition.

At the same time, he wanted one last chance at a top corporate management position. He was approached by a business-to-business transactional bartering company, and he took the job of Managing Director in May 2006. He was responsible for the U.K. market. His focus, as always, was on looking at strategy and the business plan, doing analysis, stress-testing change, executing change and refining improvements. After about a year at the company, he moved on to be Commercial Development Director at another company, which had more than 10,000 employees worldwide.

Before he started that job, though, in 2007, Geoffrey took a trip to Grand Cayman to celebrate his 40th birthday. He felt that his life had come to a crossroads, and he wanted to celebrate and reflect in one of his favourite places on earth. He loved Grand Cayman because it was home to some of his good friends and because it offered exceptional beauty and tranquility, as well as great restaurants.

One of those restaurants was owned by a friend named Neil. The restaurant, on Grand Cayman's famous Seven Mile Beach, was one of Geoffrey's favourite places to relax. He arranged to meet another friend, John, for dinner at Neil's restaurant. John was a Barbadian who had lived for many years on Grand Cayman. He was a banker, and his family owned a lot of real estate on the island. Geoffrey had a strong friendship with John, who was very charismatic and intelligent. They always enjoyed excellent conversations, and they talked about virtually any subject. John seemed to have an intuitive understanding of what Geoffrey was thinking and feeling, and Geoffrey respected John's opinion and valued his guidance.

When they met for dinner, John noticed a change in Geoffrey, who seemed quite wired and not nearly as relaxed as he usually was when he visited the island. John said to his friend, "I cannot quite understand Geoffrey, but you seem different on this visit. You just do not seem be quite yourself."

Geoffrey took a sip of his drink and looked straight at John, responding, "You are right John. I am completely unsettled, confused, even at a crossroads in my career and life. I just do not seem to be connecting with my inner ambitions. I watch people making money easily, while I need to continually work 12 to 18 hours a day just to get by. My family has deserted me, and the years have just flown by. I am not saying I have not had a successful career; after all, I am here in my favorite location on my 40th birthday having dinner with friends and drinking my favourite martini. But I do not seem to be happy."

John did not say anything in response, but his look showed that he understood what Geoffrey was saying. Before they could continue their discussion, though, Neil approached and greeted them. He wished Geoffrey a happy birthday, and then he told them to sit back and relax, that he would handle everything. A beautiful waitress named Maria came to take their drink orders. When she returned with the martini, she said, "Welcome back Geoffrey. Will you be staying long this time?" When Geoffrey replied that he would be staying about a week, Maria smiled and said, "I hope we see more of you."

When Maria left, John teased his friend about the flirtation between Geoffrey and the beautiful waitress. The mood, which had been very serious, became much more relaxed. But both John and Geoffrey knew that they would continue the conversation later.

The next day Geoffrey stopped at a local Italian coffee shop for some pastries and extra strong coffee to help get rid of the cobwebs that remained after a night of eating and drinking with friends. While he was waiting for his order, he began to reflect on his 40th birthday. He was glad he had come to Grand Cayman, where his celebration had been much more low-key and fun than it would have been if he had stayed in London.

But still, he felt that in many ways, he was unhappy. Since the death of his grandmother, he had not been close to anyone in his family. He had not been able to find and sustain a long-term romantic relationship. His major success was in the world of business – which, he realized, was also a major reason for his failure to develop other relationships. He worked very hard, traveling almost non-stop and spending long hours at his job. It seemed like only moments ago that he had been celebrating his 30th birthday, and he knew that it would be only too easy for the next 10 years to fly by, leaving him with a successful career and a healthy bank balance, but no real human connections that brought lasting happiness.

After his coffee, he set out for his daily walk on the beach and continued to consider his situation. He thought about the opportunities he had had to fall in love. In addition to Marcela and Caroline, he had had relationships with other women, but none had brought him lasting happiness. He had a friend named Tia, a beautiful woman who had been born in Hawaii. They enjoyed each other's company and even joked about getting married if they both reached the age of 60 and were still alone. But for some reason, the relationship had never moved past friendship.

Geoffrey realized that part of the problem was the pain he carried from his turbulent childhood. He was afraid to let down his defenses because he so often had been disappointed.

He had trouble trusting other people because, other than his grandparents, so many people in his childhood had broken the trust he placed in them. He was often suspicious that people had ulterior motives, even when they did not. And he usually expected people to fail to live up to his hopes and expectations for them. He rarely gave people a chance to make a mistake and then apologize and work to correct it; at the first sign of a mistake, he felt that was what he had expected all along. As a result, it was very difficult for people to get close to Geoffrey. He had lots of acquaintances, but very few real friends.

He also realized that he had pursued business success often at the expense of his personal life. He had never said no to another international trip, to putting in the late-night hours to get a proposal just right. And he often threw himself into his work as a way of avoiding getting close to people or of coping when, inevitably, they disappointed him.

Then he thought: What if this were not the case? What if he could build a business that was more balanced, that left him with time to develop other parts of his life? And what if, in this business he could build, he could work with other people who were interested in achieving the same kind of balance?

As he walked along the beach and looked out to sea, he became more and more excited about the idea. Could it be possible to achieve a balance of happiness by sharing and accomplishing together? Although much of the strategy that Geoffrey wrote in the corporate world talked extensively about teamwork, he knew that, in practice, the business world was mostly every man (or woman) for himself. Rarely were people in business willing to really help a colleague to succeed; too often they worried that the colleague's success would make them look bad. People who struggled in the business world were rarely mentored in any meaningful way. Weakness was a catalyst to remove that person rather than offering help. Furthermore, Geoffrey had never known a company executive who decided to share his bonus with the people who had helped to make it possible.

What Geoffrey was considering was a new philosophy of working that would be about sharing, encouraging others – and ultimately about trust.

Geoffrey stopped walking. He picked up some shells and dropped each one, watching it sink through the crystal clear water. He decided that he needed to take control of his own destiny. But he wanted to take control of his destiny within an environment where he was working with other people who shared his values and his belief in finding balance between work and self. He knew that would be a very difficult task, but he also felt that it was the way to find happiness.

He was very excited by this idea, but he was not sure how to start translating the idea into a workable reality. He wondered where this idea might take him, and how long it would take to get there. From a very young age, Geoffrey had been used to deciding on a course of action and then making that happen. When he was just a child and he decided to run away, he headed into the main London bus station by himself, with only his bag of coins. He left home for good at 16, and he accepted a major job at 20. He dealt with massive disappointment in his personal life, but he always kept moving forward, following a path he had set out for himself.

Now, though, he was not sure where the path was going. He decided to do what he did best: create a strategy and write a mission statement that encapsulated his thinking, philosophy and discovery.

When he got back to his hotel room, he noticed that he had several messages. John wanted to know if he cared to meet for drinks later, Maria called to say hello, and Neil asked him to stop by later that night. Geoffrey did not respond to the messages; instead, he opened his computer and started working on his mission statement.

He started by writing down his perceptions of various words. For example, he thought that confidence meant having or showing certainty; surety meant having complete trust in someone or something; respect required genuine actions based on loyalty. He considered whether people too often jumped to conclusions, analyzing a person or a situation too quickly and shallowly. He began typing as fast as he could, trying to get his thoughts down. When the telephone rang, he ignored it.

Soon he decided he was ready to write his mission statement. He began, "The journey of our people is about constant learning and sharing knowledge... Our company understands that it is the result of defining your business and then communicating it simply and in a way that engages both hearts and minds both internally and externally that will make the difference to communities that you serve."

Geoffrey realized that in order to implement this mission statement, he would have to create a company that was very different from PMI as it had been. That had been a consultancy firm with only one consultant – himself. What he wanted to do now was to create a company based on his beliefs in which he could recruit and train people with like beliefs and then work with these people to preserve this philosophy and to build a successful business. He also hoped that this company he wanted to build could serve as an example to other companies and that, if it were successful, other companies might decide to implement the same philosophy.

Although he felt like he could write forever, Geoffrey finally decided to take a break and catch up with his friends. He and John went to a local restaurant called Bed, which recently had been opened by an American entrepreneur. The bar had tables shaped like four-poster beds, and the waiters and hostesses wore pajamas.

Shortly after arriving, John noticed Maria across the bar with a friend, and he suggested that they invite the women to join them for dinner. Geoffrey realized that he was being set up, but he went along and enjoyed the evening. As John dropped him off, they made plans to meet for lunch a few days later at the yacht club.

His new project kept Geoffrey busy until the lunch appointment, and when he sat down with John, his head was still spinning with his thoughts and plans.

He said to his friend, "John you have known me for several years. In that time not only has the time disappeared into thin air, but I feel that there is more to life. I am feeling that I do not want to lose another 10 years, that there needs to be a meaningful purpose to my life, a cause. I have been thinking deeply since my arrival about the past, the present and, believe it or not, the future, I have even written a mission statement. I am not sure what all of this means — the reality of my life — but I feel it is time to open my company to truly make a difference to my life and the lives of others."

John replied, "Geoffrey, you must realize as a friend, I do not measure you or your life by milestones of achievement but by who you are as a person, how you communicate, behave and more importantly by our friendship. If you are looking for me to say you must run off and build a company because this is what you want to hear, you will not hear me say this. The most important factor here is for you to be happy, to find happiness.

"Your life is not a roadmap or a series of trips and short fixes," he said. "It should be sustained on a journey or path of success. Whatever that translates back to your personal circumstances, then this will be what is right for you in the future. Always remember you cannot replace your health or your happiness — you have no financial basis for a future without these attributes."

Geoffrey was very grateful for his friend's thoughtful support, and he knew that John truly was interested in his happiness. He also knew that his main challenge was to take the idea he had developed on Grand Cayman and turn it into the reality of a functioning, sustainable company.

Later, as he waited in the business lounge for his flight back to London, he was excited, exhilarated and nervous – and looking forward to embarking on the next stage of his life.

CHAPTER EIGHT

A Hard Lesson

"There is no education like adversity."

– Benjamin Disraeli

Paul was a businessman who had a company that specialized in oil and gas spare parts; he lived and worked in London with a country house in Lincolnshire. He and Geoffrey were friends, and Geoffrey was fascinated by Paul's mind and his ability to think creatively. When they got together, they often talked about innovation, collaboration, how to create new companies and products, and how to introduce and promote these products in Third World and emerging markets. Paul also had a huge interest in developing nations, especially in Africa, where there was no infrastructure; he had devised solutions to entering these markets, and he even had invested his own money in such programs.

After Geoffrey's return from his 40th birthday trip to Grand Cayman, he met with Paul and was explaining the thought process that had led him to decide to create a different kind of business. Geoffrey acknowledged that, although he had completed his vision for the company, he still was working out issues such as the structure and the products and services the company could offer. But he assured Paul that he was certain that he was about to embark on an exceptional journey. Paul was fascinated by Geoffrey's vision for his new company, and they talked for some time about how the company might be put together. Geoffrey enjoyed the opportunity to bounce ideas off a person whose opinion and experience he respected.

About a week later, Paul called Geoffrey and asked if Geoffrey were available to meet an associate of Paul's named

Jeremy who had flown into London from New York. Jeremy was an entrepreneur who operated two businesses; the first, which was more established, was a lottery company, and the second was a security company.

Paul told Geoffrey that Jeremy always preferred to meet at lavish places in London such as the Lanesborough Hotel in Hyde Park or the Jumeirah Hotel in Knightsbridge; this meeting was set for the Jumeirah Hotel. Paul said that Jeremy wanted to meet with Geoffrey to discuss whether there might be any opportunities for collaboration or contractual work. Paul always had spoken very highly of Jeremy, which Geoffrey found reassuring, since he had no personal knowledge of the man or his companies.

When they entered the hotel, the brass and glass doors opened to a magnificent lobby. Paul and Geoffrey walked into the lounge, which was very busy, and Paul pointed out Jeremy, who was sitting in the back of the lounge engaged in conversation. Jeremy was a tall man with a strong American accent.

Paul and Geoffrey approached and waited for Jeremy to finish his meeting. When the person to whom he was talking left, Jeremy turned to greet Paul and to meet Geoffrey. Jeremy had a strong handshake, and he struck Geoffrey as being ex-military, although Geoffrey waited for Jeremy to introduce himself and explain his reasons for wanting the meeting. Jeremy asked Paul and Geoffrey what they wanted to drink; Paul ordered tea, and Geoffrey ordered a cappuccino.

Once the drink orders had been placed, Jeremy got down to the discussion by handing Geoffrey his business card. Geoffrey noted that the card gave Jeremy's title as Chairman and CEO. Jeremy struck Geoffrey as brash and a little arrogant, but then Jeremy and Paul shared a joke, which served to break the ice a little.

Jeremy asked a lot of questions about Geoffrey's experience, his expertise and his current position. He asked if Geoffrey had any experience in security technology or in the aerospace and defense industries. Geoffrey responded that he had some experience, although he felt somewhat reluctant to reveal too much about himself and his business experience.

Part of the reason for his reluctance was that he noticed that while Jeremy was looking for a lot of information about Geoffrey, he did not seem to be very forthcoming with information about himself. He seemed to actively avoid answering questions about his circumstances and his personal life. He focused on both his lottery company and his security company, characterising them as secure and successful enterprises.

Eventually Geoffrey and Jeremy relaxed in each other's company, but nothing specific was decided before Jeremy excused himself, saying that he had another meeting. Geoffrey felt that the conversation had been interesting, but he had no idea where it might lead – or if it might lead anywhere at all.

Two months passed with no follow-up, and Geoffrey had just about written off Jeremy as an interesting discussion that had simply gone nowhere. Then his mobile rang at 8 on a cold morning and, even though the display said Unknown Number, Geoffrey answered the call.

A deep voice said, "It's Jeremy. I am sorry that I have not been in touch. I enjoyed our last meeting; could we meet again for a following discussion today or tomorrow?"

Geoffrey was surprised at the call, but after checking his schedule he told Jeremy that he had an hour free at 3 p.m. Jeremy thanked Geoffrey for being so accommodating on such short notice, adding, "I need to travel again on business, and I have a few ideas that I would like to discuss with you before I depart." They agreed to meet that day at 3 at The Ritz Hotel on Piccadilly. After hanging up with Jeremy, Geoffrey called Paul to tell him about the meeting. Paul was pleased to hear that Jeremy wanted to meet with Geoffrey again, and he asked Geoffrey to let him know how the discussion went.

When Geoffrey arrived at The Ritz 15 minutes early, Jeremy was already sitting in the main Palm Court area of the hotel. He waved Geoffrey over to his table and ordered tea. Jeremy was all smiles and jovial behavior – much different from the person Geoffrey had met two months earlier at the Jumeirah Hotel. Geoffrey was interested to see where this conversation might go.

For the first 20 minutes, Jeremy talked about his latest power boat experience and his new car. Finally Geoffrey, who was anxious to get to the purpose of the meeting, said, "I am enjoying the tea, the surroundings and the company, but I understand you are an incredibly busy person.
Exactly what would you like to discuss today?" For a moment, Jeremy seemed surprised by Geoffrey's candor, but he soon recovered and moved on to the purpose of the meeting.

Jeremy explained that he had major interests in two companies. The first was a lottery company, of which his wife was the President. The second was the security company, of which he was Chairman and CEO. He said that the President of that company was formerly with the CIA, as was the Vice

President. The other members of the management team had similar backgrounds. Jeremy said that he had several enterprises in such areas as intelligence, technology, corporate risk, crisis response, training and humanitarian support services. However, he said, "I have no structure, the management is not functioning as a company, finance and sales and marketing are a mess, and my vision is to IPO the company. Can you help?"

Geoffrey replied, "This is a very interesting proposition and not a unique set of problems. The simple answer to this question is, I can help you, but I need more information." He suggested to Jeremy that they exchange non-disclosure agreements and, once they had the NDAs, Jeremy could send him information such as his business plan and financials. When he had had a chance to study that information, Geoffrey would provide Jeremy with a review and recommendations.

Jeremy said that he was flying to the Ukraine the next day but that if Geoffrey sent him the NDA electronically that night, he would get Geoffrey the necessary information before he left on his trip. Then he suggested that they meet again after his return from the Ukraine. They agreed to meet in a week at The Jumeirah Hotel.

The NDAs were exchanged via email, and the promised information on Jeremy's company arrived just as promptly. Geoffrey read the information, and he conducted some due diligence on the company. However, he was stymied in large part because the company was set up in Nevada in the United States rather than in the U.K. But Paul had vouched for Jeremy, so Geoffrey felt reasonably confident moving forward.

He conducted an audit using the materials he had received.

Jeremy had told him that the company was a dysfunctional mess, and everything Geoffrey saw tended to support that assessment. It appeared that management had several agendas and that there was no shared vision or objective for the company – a fact that was blocking its progress. Although his audit was far from exhaustive, he had enough information to know what questions he needed answered about the company's strengths, weaknesses, opportunities and threats, and to suggest the next steps. He felt that he could listen to Jeremy's vision and translate the important points of that vision into proposals for action and that, once he got the answers he needed, he could create an outline for the first 100 days of change for the company – if Jeremy and he could agree to terms for his work.

When Jeremy returned from the Ukraine, he and Geoffrey met to discuss Geoffrey's findings. Geoffrey explained that, based on the information he had received, it probably would take him eight to 12 weeks to fully understand the position of the company and its subsidiaries. Jeremy seemed surprised by how well Geoffrey was able to understand the company in such a short time and with so little information.

Other than that, though, Jeremy had very little to say and asked very few questions of Geoffrey. Geoffrey found this odd. In his experience, most Chairmen and CEOs were prone to question and challenge the findings of outside consultants. Finally, Jeremy asked, "You believe you need a period of 18 months to restructure, build the business model and prepare for IPO?"

Geoffrey said he thought it would take that long, that there were too many intangibles for him to believe it could be done more quickly. He further cautioned Jeremy, "I do not suggest you cut corners. The very nature of building a business with longevity for the future always bases its foundations on research, planning, assessment, implementation, execution and performance management; perception is never reality."

Jeremy listened to Geoffrey's explanations and rationale, and then he dropped a bombshell. "I agree with what you are saying," he said, "but I need to go on the market within nine months."

Geoffrey was dumbfounded, but he replied, "This will be incredibly ambitious. I do not believe you have the management resources, core competencies, size of M&A targets or investment to expedite such an aggressive change program."

Jeremy smiled and said, "That is why I want to hire you."

He continued, "I am not sure how much a person like you will cost, but one thing for sure — you will pay for yourself again and again."

Jeremy asked Geoffrey to send his fee expectations, which Geoffrey did. Jeremy responded by sending Geoffrey a service contract for £10,000 more than he expected, and the offer also included class A shares in the company and a package of bonuses, medical and life insurance, and paid holidays.

Geoffrey gave termination notice for a project he was working on as a consultant for a major worldwide money transfer company. He accepted Jeremy's offer and was to begin six weeks later.

However, even though Jeremy knew that Geoffrey was still working for the other company for six weeks, he wanted Geoffrey to start immediately by being on board calls and working with the internal management of the company. As a result, Geoffrey was working practically around the clock for six weeks, trying to meet Jeremy's requirements while also finishing up with the other company. However, during the six-week introduction to Jeremy's company, Geoffrey was able to collect most of the information he needed to start the assessment and restructuring process.

Geoffrey carried out the complete SWOT analysis and, based on his research, he was able to deliver to the board a series of recommendations with a complete budget breakdown. The board accepted those recommendations with very little resistance, and Geoffrey had completed the first 100 days of his work for Jeremy.

After completing the new business plan for Jeremy's company, Geoffrey traveled to all the company offices in order to have face-to-face discussions about the new vision, mission, values and strategy for the group. He also discussed the integration of the existing companies and provided education around the new M&A targets, which were designed to raise the profile of the company enormously.

The changes were transformational. The new vision set the company in a new direction and put it on a journey from small company integration to large company acquisitions, which enabled new customer acquisitions, support services, scalability and growth.

While Geoffrey was doing this, Jeremy was managing the capital development and the two main acquisitions, which totaled approximately £60 million GBP. Jeremy also handled communication with investment banks and high-net-worth individuals. Geoffrey was never allowed to get too close to these financial dealings, but since Jeremy was a chartered accountant and a former investment banker, Geoffrey assumed this was Jeremy's area of expertise and his contribution to the business.

Geoffrey was invited to a management review meeting at which he presented the current status of objectives and explained what he had accomplished so far. He also was prepared to present his last several invoices and his expenses. Jeremy seemed to be in a very strange mood. It was clear by the balance sheet that the company had money. However, after Geoffrey was finished with his presentation, Jeremy said, "I have just turned away two sets of terms for investment. Although I know this is not the news you were expecting, I cannot agree to terms where I will lose control of the company in favor of a new shareholder. This is going to significantly impact the cash flow of the business and our creditors, but I would hope that I can pay you for your work within the next three to six months." As a gesture of good will, he offered to double Geoffrey's shareholding to 500,000 class A shares.

Geoffrey was stunned. It was clear that Jeremy was paying himself and his American counterparts a good salary, and Jeremy often bragged about his holidays to the Caribbean, his stays in five-star resorts and his visits to expensive restaurants. Yet here he was, saying he had to delay payment to the one person who was actually making critical changes and building the financial future of the company.

His surprise and displeasure were obvious to Jeremy, who made repeated promises of payment. But Geoffrey told Jeremy he needed some time to reflect on what Jeremy had said, and he left the meeting.

Geoffrey then called Paul and said that he had just had a meeting with Jeremy in which Jeremy had told him that he had no money to pay Geoffrey's invoices for the last nine months. Paul was first surprised and then angry. He asked Geoffrey to come immediately to his office so that they could discuss the situation.

When Geoffrey arrived at Paul's office an hour later, Paul met him at the door. He said, "Well young man, shall I open the Chivas Regal or shall we go to the pub?" Geoffrey smiled wryly and replied, "I think we should do both."

As Paul listened to Geoffrey's story, he was shocked. He could not believe that Jeremy would act in such an unethical way. He repeatedly asked Geoffrey, "So he has not paid you a penny?" Each time Geoffrey responded, "That is correct."

Paul said, "OK, I am trying to understand. You and Jeremy signed a service agreement for monthly fees on a schedule of payment dates, way back at the beginning of the year, correct?" Geoffrey replied, "That is correct. Can you please pour me another glass of Chivas Regal?"

Paul said, "What is strange is that Jeremy came to me around two months ago for a loan of £100,000. I thought this was a blip, and he mentioned that he was feeling bad that you had not been paid. He offered me an amazing exchange for shares in the group, so I agreed on the basis that you would receive a salary."

At this point, Geoffrey dropped his glass and put his head in his hands. "I cannot believe this," he said. "Paul, why did you not tell me about this conversation?"

Paul replied, "I thought that the conversation was best kept between Jeremy and myself. But now I see that there is more to this setup and operation that I should know about before there is any further damage."

Then Paul asked Geoffrey what he planned to do.

Geoffrey said that he was not sure what he should do next. He had taken a huge hit to his savings, and without payment from Jeremy, he was running low on money. He said, "I have really enjoyed working on Jeremy's project, and I had no idea that he was going to forfeit payment to key members of his staff. There was evidence that he was certainly spending money, and it's obvious by what you have told me that this money was from you."

Paul replied, "He took money from me, but he may have taken investment from many people. It appears to me that this money was fueling his lifestyle; he always appeared to be a player."

Then Paul turned his focus to the bigger picture. "The truth is the only conviction in life, and it self-evident that the truth has arrived just in time," he said. "Consider this a learning experience. You are fortunate to escape and young enough to dust yourself down and start again.

"I will help you where I can," he said. "You are bigger than this, Geoffrey and better than the man who has tried to drag you down. He will not succeed. He will have to be answerable one day."

Geoffrey realized that there was a lot of truth in what Paul said. This certainly had been a painful lesson. Still, he had enjoyed the experience of working in a new sector and supporting the further development of a company that was quite clearly unorganized. He knew that without strong core management, a strong delivery team and a solid product and service offerings, sales contracts and a robust business model, no company could succeed. He also realized that he had provided Jeremy's company with a blueprint and had taken the company a good part of the way down the road toward achieving these goals.

He also thought about this experience in terms of the type of company he had decided to build while he walked on the beach in Grand Cayman. Jeremy's enterprise was the exact opposite of that company. First, it lacked organization, a plan for achieving success and people committed to implementing and continually evaluating the plan and revising it as necessary.

More importantly, the company he wanted to create was built on honesty and ethical conduct. His experience with Jeremy convinced him anew of the need for a business to have a culture built on sharing. Jeremy had not shared the assets of the company, keeping them to support his own lifestyle rather than honoring his contracts. But, Geoffrey thought, sharing meant more than that. It meant sharing knowledge, sharing resources and having a common vision of the mission of the company. It also meant sharing a value system or a culture based on doing what is right and ethical.

Geoffrey knew that the time had come to act on the mission he had composed in Grand Cayman. Only by creating the company he had envisioned there could he gain control of his own destiny and make his own way in the world. He did not know exactly where this journey would lead, but he was prepared to commit to starting the journey. He was ready to launch a company in which he could call on the knowledge and skills he had developed over the previous 18 years and work with like-minded people who shared his vision and his goals.

He and Paul talked for a long time, until Paul finally said, "Geoffrey I really need to go home now. But first I need to ask you, have you decided what's next?"

Geoffrey smiled and said, "Yes, Paul. This is the beginning of my new life. I am going to start a company based on shared values, skills and competencies, and a shared vision. I need to be a leader who reflects those values through everything I do as a single person and within a team. I will try not to let a situation like this happen to me again or affect the people around me. Situations like this should not happen in life."

Paul smiled and said, "You will learn that situations like this do happen in life, and all too often You will need to deal with many more situations with people like Jeremy. But you have learned one of life's important lessons, and from this you can prosper and grow."

CHAPTER NINE

Building a Dream

"Far and away the best prize that life offers is the chance to work hard at work worth doing."

– Theodore Roosevelt

On a September morning in 2007, Geoffrey arrived at Heathrow for a business trip to Johannesburg, South Africa. He went to the British Airways business lounge and was getting himself an espresso when he heard someone say, "Hello, Geoffrey."

When he turned, he was surprised to see Stephen, who was an associate and former client. Geoffrey had met Stephen in many countries all over the world, but never in London. They began to talk and discovered that both of them were going to Johannesburg, and they agreed to meet for dinner once they arrived and settled in.

Geoffrey met Stephen when Stephen was a successful program manager with British Telecom and Geoffrey was working with British Telecom on some large international programs. Since then, Stephen's responsibilities had shifted to consultancy and assisting U.K. companies wishing to market their products and services internationally. Stephen also worked with some smaller companies on benchmarking performance and supporting channel and vertical sales objectives.

Geoffrey always enjoyed talking and sharing ideas with Stephen. He found that Stephen often helped him work more creatively on problems, and he was anxious to discuss his plans for his new company with his friend.

On the 13-hour flight, Geoffrey continued to think about the company he was planning to launch. He considered what types of people he should recruit, the business model he should establish, and the customers he should focus on serving. He knew that in order to have a successful launch, it was critical to do extensive planning and research. Based on his many years in corporate life, Geoffrey knew that a company's strategies and methodologies are only as good as the people who implement and execute them. He also knew that a business depends on the quality of its offerings and that it needs to generate money; it cannot rely on its initial seed money.

One of Geoffrey's favorite quotes was by the American essayist Hamilton Wright Mabie, who said: "The question for each man to settle is not what he would do if he had means, time, influence and educational advantages; the question is what he will do with the things he has. The moment a young man ceases to dream or to bemoan his lack of opportunities and resolutely looks his conditions in the face, and resolves to change them, he lays the corner stone of a solid and honorable success." Geoffrey was determined to lay the corner stone of such a success with his new company.

When Geoffrey arrived at his hotel, he already had a message from Stephen suggesting that they have dinner the following evening at one of Geoffrey's favorite restaurants in Johannesburg.

He sent Stephen a quick note confirming, and then he retired for the night. He was in Johannesburg on behalf of a telecom client, and he had five very hectic days of meetings. A programmer from the company was due to arrive the next day to help with the project.

His meetings the next day began at 7:30 a.m. and continued until 6. He planned to shower and collect his thoughts before meeting Stephen for dinner at 8, but when he got to his room he found that the message light on his phone was blinking and several envelopes had been slid under his door. He decided to deal with the messages after he showered, but while he was showering he heard his room phone and then his mobile ring, and finally there was a knock on the door. He put on a robe and answered the door, finding it was the programmer. She suggested that they have dinner and talk about the project, but he told her he already had plans for dinner and suggested instead that they meet back at the hotel at 9:30. He then called Stephen and rescheduled dinner for 7:30.

When Geoffrey arrived at the restaurant, he and Stephen were seated at a table. Geoffrey began to explain what he had been thinking over the last year or so. He told Stephen about the plans he had developed on the beach at Grand Cayman, how he had worked for nine months for a client who did not pay him, and how he was preparing to launch his new company. Stephen listened carefully, and then he asked, "What will this new entity offer and consist of?"

"My thought is to create a strategic consultancy with keen entrepreneurial thinking based on a team of successful people who share the same values." Geoffrey replied. "It is very easy to set up a company, but the true value lies in the people, the experience and the offering. This new venture needs to offer a wealth of business foresight, keen insight and experiences in research and analysis, strategy and planning, process development, business communications and performance management.

"If this company is founded, it will need to have a strong

emphasis and belief in the philosophy and principles of business intelligence, experience-based solutions and integrated cross-discipline solutions. It needs to demonstrate a track record of working on challenges within some of the top Fortune 500 organizations, and delivering integrated people solutions with effective business processes and relevant targeted communications.

"Importantly, the company will need to grow based on experienced personnel; a nucleus of individuals with complementary skills, expertise and experience; a professional infrastructure; proactive communications; and an organized and proficient staff that will meet goals and deadlines and that will provide a successful platform for winning together," Geoffrey concluded.

Stephen asked Geoffrey to talk further about the mission statement he had drawn up in Grand Cayman. Geoffrey explained that he believed that his company should involve constant learning and sharing knowledge among its people. He also believed that it is only by understanding your business, defining that business and then communicating that simply and in a way that engages both hearts and minds, that a company can make a difference to the communities it serves.

He concluded, "This awakening makes complete sense in terms of my moral beliefs. I want to open a company where I can recruit, train and develop people, and where I have guardianship over the integrity of the brand, philosophy, culture and actions of others."

Stephen grew excited listening to Geoffrey talk. "I think this is amazing Geoffrey," he said, adding, "I can think of many compelling services that I could bring to the proposition:

analysis of business flows, market segmentation, sector analysis, market modeling, risk analysis, simulation, strategic planning, strategic scenarios, market research, distribution analysis, business process reengineering, customer satisfaction measurement, product and service definition, launch planning, team dynamics and profiling, programmer team selection, project and programme planning and management, sales force planning, territory planning, compensation planning, incentive programmes, account management training, channel management and network marketing."

Geoffrey said that adding those to the list of core service propositions he already had developed would create an incredible range of capabilities. "My original thoughts were to have a division for consultancy and programme management, and a division for business planning and investor readiness," he said. Then looking at Stephen across the table, Geoffrey asked, "Would you like to join me in the business? I would really be honored if you would join me. I am looking for a trusted individual to head up and run the consultancy and programme management division."

Stephen was stunned by the offer, but he did not take long to think about it. "I would be delighted," he said. "What are the next steps?"

Geoffrey said he was still trying to decide on a name. He liked using PMI, the name he had used for his earlier consultancy; the letters would stand for Performance Management International. Stephen said he also liked the name, so it was settled.

Then Geoffrey noted that while they had the name and a general outline of the mission statement and values, there was still a lot of strategic work to do to define the company's goals and objectives; its strengths, weaknesses, opportunities and threats (SWOT); and its strategic action plan, sales and marketing plan, financial plan and business model. Stephen and Geoffrey agreed that they would meet when there were both back in London to start that strategic work. Then Geoffrey excused himself for his meeting with the programmer.

Back in London, Geoffrey and Stephen began to work on the details of launching PMI. Geoffrey already had ideas for a presentation introducing the company that he planned to send to 10 contacts with whom he already had done business. Based on the feedback from this presentation, they would launch the website, digital online campaign and a company day event to introduce the full offering to a combination of associates, colleagues and clients.

Geoffrey knew that, in order to prepare for the launch, he and Stephen needed to develop the right products and service offering, identify the model market, evaluate the current state of the industry and their competition, consider what the future market might be, and use that information to identify the niche opportunity for their new company.

They met at Stephen's home in the Berkshire countryside; their objective was to define the full approach of change consultancy and to establish a business plan and tool kits for investors. They started with Geoffrey's core idea that the foundation of a company was an understanding of the role it plays in an overall business, sales, and marketing and communication strategy. The goal was to define a brand or goal in a way that moves both employees and clients, and to communicate that effectively. In order to do that, it is critical to have a deep understanding of the role sales, marketing and communications strategy play within a company's overall business.

Stephen and Geoffrey noted that while a consultant always asks for information from the client in order to diagnose problems and find solutions, the quest is to find the information that really matters. This quest was the basic role of a consultant, they decided. Then Geoffrey asked, "What words can we associate with the letters that make up the word *quest*?"

After some brainstorming, they came up with these words: Qualities, Understanding, Expertise, Strategic Thinking, and Time.

Geoffrey said to Stephen, "If you think strategically about what are the most significant underlying factors that affect business performance, it is clear that employee motivation impacts customer behavior, and customer behavior needs to be positive in the relationship to secure new contracts, vertical sale opportunities and business referrals, so maintaining and increasing the motivation of the client companies we work with is valuable."

Stephen suggested that they expand on these ideas to broaden their definitions of the work *quest*, thereby creating a model they could use in executive board reviews and management workshops. They worked through the day and created these definitions:

Q is for Qualities. When managers are asked what qualities they most want their team members to bring to a given project, they may generate a list that includes responsibility, integrity, initiative, creativity, task orientation, persistence, clarity, co-operation, etc. These qualities exist in every company, and this is where potential skills arise. Which qualities would you like to see more of in yourself? Which would others on your team like to see more of, or less of? Learning to access and express any specific quality or attribute is one kind of learning goal.

U is for Understanding. Understanding requires more than just information; it requires a comprehension of all the components of a particular subject or system and the relationships among these components. You can have a great deal of information about a job or task without really understanding it. You may be able to state the mission of the company or of a given project, but do you really understand the mission sufficiently to be truly effective? You should ask yourself: Given your current performance goals what, if understood better, would make success easier or more likely? Such goals might be stated in terms of, for example, "Expand my understanding of…" (my co-workers, my boss, the customers, the competition, market dynamics, systems and processes, finance, obstacles, and so on).

E is for Expertise. Expertise is what you call know-how or skill. It can be technical or emotional. Ask yourself what skills you have or could develop that would let you attain a higher level of performance. What skills are you learning that you could apply to your present role or project? Which of these skills could you learn from experience on the job, and which require some book or classroom learning? Skills you could choose to develop might include computer literacy skills, negotiating skills, communication skills, accounting skills, technical skills, management or leadership skills, or you could choose to master a given body of knowledge. Once you develop these skills, they are available for you in a wide variety of future tasks.

S is for Strategic Thinking: Strategic thinking can be viewed as a quality, a skill, or an understanding. But it is a distinct kind of thinking. It is the ability to step back from the trees and see the forest, to see past short-term goals and view long-range objectives. It is a critical skill not just for a few managers and leaders, but for everyone in the organisation. You need to ask yourself: How strategically am I thinking? Do I have a strategic perspective, or merely a tactical view? How clear are my priorities in the company? Are my current activities in line with my long-term objectives? Am I thinking independently enough? Is my work life balanced and in harmony with the rest of my life? Is my definition of work self-driven? Do I see tasks in relation to other projects being completed? Do I see what has to be done in line with the overall mission of the team and company? Do I think strategically about my life? Strategic thinking is about more than setting goals and targets in your work and in your life; it is about developing the ability to think strategically whenever you need to.

T is for Time: All work is done in time and related to time, and understanding this relationship is critical to successful work. The best strategies and the best experts have failed because of an inability to come to terms with this fact. Do you complete your work on time? How aware are you of the time required to complete the tasks on your to-do-list? Are you feeling constantly pressured by time? Are you constantly behind on time lines? Do you procrastinate? You may want to consider setting a learning goal around the relationship between time, task and priorities.

The whole idea of QUEST was to provide leadership through dialogue and discussion, to ask questions and to promote discussion and creative thinking around those questions, and thus to help leaders broaden their horizons and persuade others within the mission to do the same.

Geoffrey and Stephen knew that successful companies often decide to build on their success by bringing in additional capital and/or shareholders. When a company's management takes this step, it takes on new challenges. Most boards spend much of their time concerned with cash flow and liquidity. However, there are many other things boards need to understand and direct, including sustainability, corporate social responsibility, protection of data and intellectual property, public relations, corporate manslaughter, crisis management, mediation to reduce conflict, due diligence, and audits. The QUEST model was designed to help management understand key questions and identify gaps in the organization. Stephen and Geoffrey agreed that if clients had a structured process for addressing and managing these kinds of questions on a regular basic, it would go a long way toward mitigating various risks.

Geoffrey said, "We can call this program PMI Performance

Assurance, as it reflects proactive leadership to ensure a company is not only conscious of these risks but has built into its process management continual monitoring and pre-planned responses to any potentially adverse impact."

Throughout the afternoon, Geoffrey and Stephen continued to build on the vision for PMI, including research and analysis, strategy and planning, process development, business communications, and performance management.

When they were finished, they had designed a company that was about expert performance, that would enable companies to calibrate and measure performance before execution, and that could ensure that every decision a company made considered reputation, the budget, shareholders, its clients and the market.

It was clear that PMI could now manage effective services that identified a company's objectives, the gaps in the skill set and organizational structure, the target sectors and infrastructure, the profile of transactions, the economics of the current methods used and the distribution of the daily balances.

The delivery phase enabled PMI to thoroughly test a company and project to validate a sound user experience, develop training programs for internal company programs, support marketing and communications to define channel management and requirements, build communications and launch plans across vertical channels, and performance manage its work.

The objective was to redefine the way that a company was presented, to build and support a market-leading brand through unique and compelling experiences, to differentiate a company's competitive advantages, to increase a company's impact and appeal, and to establish a platform for market development, all the while maximizing sales performance and return on investment.

CHAPTER TEN

Launching a Company

"To business that we love, we rise betime and go to't with delight."

– William Shakespeare

The next step was to discuss how PMI could help a company prepare to raise capital and pursue business growth. Stephen said, "The model we have discussed so far is very powerful. But what happens if we meet a company that requires our services for business growth? Suppose they cannot afford to hire our services until the company realizes a transaction?"

Geoffrey thought for a few minutes, and then he suggested, "We can serve such businesses through the side of our company that focuses on business planning and investor readiness."

They began to discuss how this side of the business might work. Geoffrey noted that the first step in raising capital is to draft a capital plan for the growth of a business. The company then can use this plan to identify its funding requirements in terms of the amount, the timing, the structure as well as the most appropriate capital mix for business growth. The plan also should look into alternatives to raising external capital.

"By defining a company's business objectives and strategies, we can identify all the costs involved in a company's business growth plans, including working capital requirements as well as the impact of budget over-runs and product development delays. Then we can look long and hard at the feasibility of the proposition," Geoffrey said, adding, "The capital plan might need to be revisited once the business plan is completed, as this is likely to identify additional issues and risk."

Stephen said, "So this way we could determine what resources a company would require to grow its business, when the resources are needed, how to obtain them — whether they can be sourced from within the business – as well as what the objectives would be and the value of the equity in the business would be following the introduction of new capital."

"Precisely," Geoffrey responded. "Attracting equity investment is not an easy process. Businesses need to be well-prepared and investment-ready to maximise the potential for success. A failure to be investment-ready is the most common barrier to accessing equity investment. Second chances are rare, so it is important to become investment-ready before establishing relationships with potential investors, regardless of a company's stage of development or capital needs.

"Investors may be found among friends and family, venture capitalists, financial institutions and business angels, but wherever the capital is found, we can offer companies this service: to help them become investment-ready," he said.

Although Stephen was not as experienced as Geoffrey in this area, he quickly saw how this part of their business fit perfectly with the part they already had designed. He noted that when investors put their money into a company, what they are investing in is not really a specific product or service, because there almost always are many companies that can produce that product or provide that service. Instead, what they are investing in is the capability of that specific company and its people.

"We are in the people business, and this idea we are discussing would take us from ideas to features to value to sales to investment opportunity," he said. "But could we operate a consultancy side of the business and an investor readiness side?"

Geoffrey replied, "If you think about the strategic proposition, you have the ability to maximize the services or products you work with for any one client because consultancy is short-lived. It's not like the old days, when you might well win a 12-month revolving project. Now most consultancy deals are project by project. However, the board and management will respect the creation of a business plan for the company or investment. In fact, we can create corporate and investor tool boxes and have consultancy work in pre-planning, during the project and after the delivery of the business plan."

Geoffrey began to list the issues that a business must address as it works to become investment-ready. These issues include:

- Management capacity and systems
- A suitable business structure (usually a company)
- A realistic business valuation
- Management commitment
- A business model
- An investment structure, terms sheet and exit plan
- A business and/or commercialisation plan
- An investment proposal (information memorandum) and pitch
- Management capacity and systems.

He added that the balance of skills and experience needed to grow a business changes as a business moves through its life cycle. Not all businesses seeking to attract equity investment have the necessary skills and experience to undertake the range of activities needed to grow the business. He suggested that gaps in those skills and that experience could be identified and addressed through the QUEST model by one or a combination of the following:

- Recruiting personnel with the necessary skills
- Appointing a board that has the required skills and experience
- Purchasing expert advice.
- A suitable business structure.

"There is a lot of work in training and in the development of others," he said. "Investors will want a commitment from management that when the going gets tough, management will not just walk away. We will need to develop the following areas of strategy:"

- The business model, which shows investors how the business will make money. It contains a description of how the business operates and how it will generate revenue and profits. A business model for an Internet-based business will be different from a business model for a manufacturing business.
- Investment structure, term sheet and exit plan. Investors need to know how the investment will be structured and how they will realise a return on their investment. The term sheet identifies how much capital is required, what it will be used for, when it will be needed and how much

equity is on offer. There also must be an exit strategy, because investors will want to know how they can get their funds out of the business. A company's strategy may be a trade sale, a management buyout, listing on a stock market or obtaining another investor. But companies usually are reluctant to pay back investors in the very early stages.

- Business and commercialisation plan. The business plan describes the opportunity as well as how and why it will be realized. If the investment proposal involves the commercialisation of a new product or service, then a commercialisation plan also should be developed.
- PMI Tool Box. This would include an investment teaser, investor PowerPoint, executive summary and one-page offer document or investment brief that outlines the investment opportunity by capturing the key points that will encourage an investor to seek more information. An investment pitch needs to be planned and well prepared.

Finally, Geoffrey outlined the sources of investment capital, which include:

Family and Friends

Family and friends are an important source of capital and one of the only sources available for early-stage businesses development. Before pursuing this approach, the business should consider the risk of failure and the impact that failure could have on the principals' ongoing relationship with family and friends who have invested in the business. Generally, the degree of investment readiness needed will be less rigorous with family and friends than with other sources of capital. However, all arrangements should be formalised.

Business Angels

These are usually high-net-worth individuals with cash resources to invest in a high-growth business that has the potential to offer high returns. The level of risk the investor will accept and involvement in the business the investor will require varies from one investor to another. But generally, business angels invest in companies that they feel have a potential for growth and that they believe will provide them with a substantial return on their investment.

They often have an active involvement in the development of the business, bringing skills, experience, contacts and networks as well as funds. They can provide funds during all stages of the business life cycle, investing over the long term – usually three to 10 years – in amounts that usually range between £100,000 and £1 million to £2 million.

Usually they invest in geographic locations that allow them to be actively involved in the business. Angel investors are one of the few sources of early-stage (seed) capital, but they more often invest at the post-seed stage.

Angel investment is largely an informal investment process, but estimates of the level of investment flows through this process are significant — greater than £1 billion per annum. But while angel investment is an important source of capital, it is often difficult to identify and access. Angel investors can be found through business contacts or networks and advisors such as accountants, lawyers and specialist consultants.

Venture Capital

Venture capitalists are specialist financial intermediaries who seek high returns from investing in relatively high-risk companies. Most will expect to take an active and influential role in the development of a business and may be more hard-nosed about seeking an exit by selling their investment in a given time frame. Investment levels are in the order of £1 million to £10 million or more and are likely to be staged according to the achievement of agreed-upon milestones. Generally, venture capitalists favor businesses with a successful operating history of several years.

Raising capital through a venture capital company normally takes three to nine months. A business seeking investment will need sufficient funds to continue operations for about 12 months.

The rate of return sought by the investor will depend on the level of risk; it would be higher for an investment in a start-up company than for a business in the expansion stage. Venture capitalists usually require at least 25 per cent per annum over the life of the investment.

Venture capitalists typically invest in less than 2 per cent of projects presented to them and might spend less than one minute on the initial assessment of a proposal that comes across their desk. It is important for a business to present its case in a way that maximises the chance that it will get serious consideration. Venture capitalists qualify potential investors based on their preferences and availability of capital; not all venture capital funds have money available for start-up investments.

Some of the factors that make a company attractive to investment capitalists and other potential sources of capital include having experienced and effective management with a proven track record; being in a high-growth sector and having high growth potential; having a replicable business model; having strong financial returns; having a competitive advantage; having customers as demonstrated by a strong sales history or confirmed purchase intentions; having exceptional market knowledge and distribution systems; and having a clear exit strategy.

Once they felt they were well on their way to understanding how they were going to set up and position their company, Geoffrey contacted 10 large corporations and 10 small to midsize businesses. All 10 of the large clients, which were all Fortune 100 companies, responded, and Geoffrey set up meetings with each in the U.K. and overseas; it seemed that their business cards could not be printed and their server could not be installed fast enough to meet the demand. The meetings yielded 10 briefings for consultancy, and Stephen and Geoffrey were busy responding to due dates for submissions. Although they had planned to focus on smaller companies, it soon became clear that landing one large corporate client would be enough to see them through their first year.

Then, about a month after the mailers had been sent out, they got a response from one of the small to mid-size businesses. Lawrence from RWE called Geoffrey asking for some assistance in business planning. RWE became PMI's first official client – and the test case for the strategy that had been developed for the company.

RWE supplied security products and was seeking funding for the rapid growth opportunity identified within its five-year plan; this would require not just money but also a sound management team. First, PMI did a complete analysis and identified ways in which the company needed to remake itself in order to be in a position to take advantage of the opportunity for growth. PMI identified key positions and helped recruit and train the best people to fill those positions. They also helped reconfigure the company's cash management process so that it allowed funds to be distributed properly and in a way that synchronised the production flow and mix to satisfy the demand from the sales groups and that allowed for high demand and rapid growth.

Most of RWE's larger clients provided RWE products to their customers as a customer service or added security for their property. PMI helped RWE define the most appropriate marketing approach to address the large-volume prospects, thereby enhancing sales productivity and direct registrations on the network.

To support the new management process, PMI delivered to the management team a new organisational structure with defined resource levels; clear roles, responsibilities and training; and new methods of performance management. In addition, focused training and coaching helped the whole team develop an integrated service ethic to deliver the most effective and sensitive service to their clients at any time and in any place.

Then PMI used its considerable experience, its network of key resources and management coaching to help RWE convince potential investors not only of the strength of the opportunity but also of the company's enthusiastic, purposeful management team. Continuing support from PMI enabled the management team not only to achieve the required fund raising but also to design, build and manage an effective organisation to deliver their own aggressive plan and eventually lead to stock market placement consideration

Interestingly, despite the initial burst of interest from the big companies, PMI did not get any business from those firms. There were discussions about projects, but those discussions always were derailed by issues such as timing, procurement or corporate reorganisation. It became clear that PMI's niche was going to be in the small to midsize market.

Two other projects that surfaced after the RWE job came from Geoffrey's old friend Paul. In the first, Paul had a friend named Frederick who lived in Toulouse, France. Frederick, who was a well-known scientist, was developing a new vaccine. But his work was very unfocused, and Paul asked Geoffrey to visit the lab in Toulouse to assess the situation. Paul had invested heavily in the project, and he was beginning to worry about losing his money.

Upon visiting the lab and talking with Frederick, Geoffrey determined that the scientist was uncomfortable leaving his lab. Geoffrey suggested to Paul that Frederick should work with a local hospital to support him and help him further develop his work so that the vaccine could become a commercial possibility.

Paul also asked Geoffrey to travel to Nigeria, where Paul was considering making some investments. Paul wanted Geoffrey to talk to some people in Nigeria and determine whether such an investment would be a good idea.

After a week in Nigeria, Geoffrey returned to the U.K. and reported to Paul that, although there might be many business opportunities available in Nigeria, he felt that they carried too much risk compared with the potential for reward. Based on that report, Paul decided to focus his investing in other alternative markets.

CHAPTER ELEVEN

Finding a Path

"I've learned that making a living is not the same thing as making a life."

– Maya Angelou

After getting off to a good start, business began to slow down for PMI. Existing clients were constantly demanding more delivery across increasingly complex issues, objectives were getting larger, and fees were barely covering the company's costs. Geoffrey and Stephen were pitching for new consultancy projects, but many of these pitches did not seem to go anywhere. Geoffrey was frustrated, but he still believed that things would turn around. All they needed was one big project.

At this point, Paul was in discussion with some large European businessmen who needed some support in the start-up, development and management of a large project involving humanitarian support and agriculture export from mainland Europe to Iraq. Paul recommended that they contact Geoffrey and his team to discuss the project.

Not long afterward, Geoffrey got a call on his mobile phone as he was walking along the River Thames. The person on the other end of the phone, who had a strong Dutch accent, said, "My name is Gerhard, and my family has been in business since 1890 in Holland. We started in the shipping and fishing business, supplying fish to the European and Middle East markets, and we expanded into the supply of poultry, construction and then oil and gas. We now have an opportunity to develop a full-service international country rehabilitation company to supply agriculture, rural development, transport and logistics, oil and gas, energy services, industrial production and educational development to Iraq. We have spent much time speaking to Paul about his involvement in the program, and he suggested that we speak with you."

Geoffrey was very excited; he knew that a project like this could be just the game-changer that PMI needed. He replied, "Gerhard, this sounds like a remarkable project. In fact, what you are describing is an agriculture development program. The scope of opportunity sounds immense. Do you have a business plan or materials to review?"

Gerhard laughed and said, "That is why I need the services of your firm. When can we meet?"

They arranged a meeting for the following week. Geoffrey called Stephen to let him know about this development. Next, he called Paul to thank him for the referral and to ask if Paul had any information on Gerhard and his business. Paul promised to make some enquiries and get back to Geoffrey.

Paul did gather some information on Gerhard's business activities in Holland from the Dutch Chamber of Commerce. The documents showed that he was in business, he was late on some of his accounting, but that there were no adverse historical activities on any of the companies he controlled or was associated with. That helped to put Geoffrey's mind at ease.

When the meeting date arrived, Geoffrey and Stephen got to the meeting 30 minutes early, thinking they could use the time to settle in and finish their final preparations for the meeting. Much to their surprise, though, they found Gerhard and his father already waiting.

After introductions and greetings, Geoffrey and Stephen told the two men about PMI, its philosophy and its capabilities. Gerhard seemed impressed, and then it was his turn to talk about his company.

He said that earlier in 2009 he had launched a company called Banner International, Inc., which was the holding company for a privately owned group of companies. It was a full-service international country rehabilitation company that provided agriculture and rural development; transport and logistics; oil, gas and energy services; industrial production; and educational development to post-war and Third World countries. Banner's strategic objective was to become, through organic growth and acquisition, a leading provider of international country rehabilitation services to governments, government agencies and NGOs.

Gerhard said that the key objective of Banner's services was the prevention of poverty and hunger. To that end, Banner offered a complete range of both proactive and reactive mission-critical services. It worked through a collaborative network of trusted strategic partners to deliver these services.

Then Gerhard said, "We have created a new company but require the expert services of a company like PMI to support us across structure, management and investment opportunities. We see this as a partnering opportunity, and we are prepared to pay for your services but urgently need to formalize a structure around business sustainability and growth."

He asked Geoffrey and Stephen, "Where do you believe you can help Banner?"

Geoffrey responded, "The first priority needs to create a business plan around the objectives and risks of the business. This is an immense opportunity, but if the correct planning is not carefully managed, you could fail before you have delivered."

He then said that PMI could support Banner with a range of services, including:

- Execute full IPR, company registration and trade mark protection
- Direct company operations to meet budget and other financial goals
- Direct short-term and long-range planning and budget development to support strategic business goals
- Establish the performance goals, allocate resources, and assess policies for senior management
- Demonstrate successful execution of business strategies for company products and services
- Direct and participate in acquisition and growth activities to support overall business objectives and plans
- Participate in capital market development, including participation in road shows, bank meetings, analyst meetings and more
- Develop, establish and direct execution of operating policies to support overall company policies and objectives
- Define the appropriate marketing organization for the company's maturity/size
- Create modeling for the company culture and growth development
- Conduct strategic planning, including channel management support, corporate positioning market and competitive analysis, customer segment selection and penetration plans, and related product positioning

- Oversee marketing communications, including branding, public relations, advertising, white papers, trade shows, seminars and events collateral materials, analyst and market research management, and website design and content either directly or on an outsourced basis
- Define and direct marketing programs for demand creation, lead generation and interface for lead tracking and management
- Develop and manage channel and partner strategies and programs
- Develop product management including market and customer research for market and product requirements
- Interface with Board of Directors and senior management for product development, product pricing and product life-cycle management
- Develop product marketing, including product launch management, sales training, presentations, sales tools, competitive analysis and general sales support
- Work with the Board of Directors and the other executive team members to identify and develop strategic alliances
- Raise venture/public financing
- Communicate with board members
- Close/grow major customer accounts
- Develop and manage the company's entire marketing budget
- Develop and track metrics and success criteria for all marketing programs and activities
- Act as spokespersons.

"PMI also has the ability to bring outside partners to

support the company in areas such as legal and strategic tax partners, investment and venture capital funding, executive and senior management board recruitment, business transformation and change management, conflict and mediation management, and business sustainability," Geoffrey said.

Gerhard and his father were impressed by what they heard, and they asked how they might structure an agreement with PMI. Geoffrey said that they would draw up a proposal covering the first 100 days of the engagement and have it to them the next day. They agreed, and they left to return to Holland.

Geoffrey and Stephen were excited to being work on the proposal. To help them draw it up, Geoffrey called a friend of his named Nigel, who was a risk director for a major company and therefore had lots of experience in risk analysis, senior company board reviews and business sustainability and audit. Geoffrey felt that it would be good to get an outside perspective on the project, especially since he and Stephen desperately wanted it to work because the company needed the influx of cash.

Nigel met with Geoffrey and Stephen to examine the scope of the project. After a long discussion, they decided that PMI would need to deliver 257 projects both internally and through its associated partners with a total delivery team of 45 people over a 200-day period. Stephen transferred this information into the promised 100-day plan, complete with a GANTT chart detailing the full scope of work, the objectives and the resources. Under the plan, Geoffrey would be interim CEO for Banner, which would take him away from PMI.

Geoffrey and Stephen discussed the impact of this absence on PMI, and they concluded that the income the Banner project would bring in would more than compensate for any loss to PMI because of losing the services of Geoffrey for a time.

They wrote up the proposal and sent the document; under the terms of the proposal, Banner would retain PMI for a period of 100 days, and the contract would renew automatically unless Banner decided to terminate it. About 10 days after they sent the proposal, Gerhard called to accept and to ask Geoffrey to start work immediately.

The plan was for Geoffrey to work full time on the Banner project, leaving Stephen to sustain the existing PMI contracts and grow that business. After the first 100 days, Banner renewed the contract for another 100 days.

At this point, Geoffrey had issued three monthly invoices, which had not been paid. He had fielded some calls from PMI partners who were worried about payment, and he had had several calls with Gerhard, who told Geoffrey to re-send the invoices and that he would receive payment shortly.

After 180 days of work, Geoffrey was beginning to get seriously concerned about Banner's ability to pay for the work PMI had done. The money owed had reached about £300,000, and Gerhard's response was that he was sorry for the delay but that payment would be made before Christmas.

Geoffrey made a call on 10 December 2009, and Gerhard said he was traveling to Iraq but would be back in Holland on or before 15 December, and that his father was scheduled to make the payment. At this point, Geoffrey began to panic, wondering how his young company could survive if the payment from Banner never came.

Paul called to ask Geoffrey over for holiday drinks, and he immediately recognized that there was something wrong. Reluctantly, Geoffrey explained the situation. He told Paul that he had not been paid, even though he had delivered on more than 250 projects, that he had more than 45 people working on this project non-stop, and that on behalf of Banner he had made job offers for a number of positions with Banner, including CFO, COO, head of Marketing, head of Business Development, head of Partner and Acquisitions, and head of Risk Management. Paul was stunned and asked Geoffrey to come to his offices immediately.

Geoffrey went to Paul's office, and he was nearly in tears. He said to his friend, "After what happened with Jeremy, how can I be left with this mess? I am finished."

Paul asked him what he was going to do, and Geoffrey replied that he was trying to figure out a plan for damage control. Stephen was familiar with Holland, so he was going to visit Gerhard's offices there and see what he could find out about where the man was and what his circumstances were. At that point, Geoffrey said, they would have to decide on a next step.

Paul was concerned for the well-being of his friend, and he asked Geoffrey how he was doing after such a difficult year. Geoffrey replied, "You can see how much weight I have lost. I sold the house at the beginning of the year and put my possessions into storage, putting the proceeds from the sale into the business in what was initially a loan to PMI. I have been fortunate enough to stay with some very dear friends and continue operating the company, which has reduced my overhead and allowed me to continue.

"I never believed that I could end up a second time in this

position. You certainly have some interesting business associates, Paul," he said ruefully. "But the million-dollar question is where I go from here. Regretfully, I need to dust myself down and look to the New Year, but I have no idea how to explain the disappearance of Gerhard to my employees, associates and investors – or more importantly to let them know how or when they will be paid."

Paul replied, "Gerhard's actions are completely immoral and unacceptable. He cannot get away with this forever, and he will re-appear, I have an associate you need to meet in January. He is a Russian oligarch, very influential, and I know he can help."

Then Paul left the room briefly and returned with an envelope. He handed it to Geoffrey and said, "Pay me when you are back on your feet. Do not consider it a loan, just friendship."

Geoffrey did not know what to say; words could not express his gratitude. He realized that this was the biggest challenge he had faced so far, and he knew that the envelope was a sign of Paul's support and his belief that Geoffrey could get through this and be even stronger.

Geoffrey and Stephen spent the following days assessing the damage that Gerhard and his father had caused to their business. They made calls to their associates, and they took time to reflect on what to do next.

On Boxing Day, Geoffrey received an email from Gerhard wishing him a happy Christmas and new year. Geoffrey was stunned, and although he immediately emailed back, he received no response. He also tried calling Gerhard, but the phone number was disconnected.

The next day, Stephen visited Gerhard's office – and he found it chained up. A security guard told him that Gerhard had not been working from that office in months. In fact, the guard thought Stephen was a potential buyer for the building. That convinced Stephen and Geoffrey that they needed to focus on resetting PMI's resources and devising a new strategy to drive performance and cash flow for the next quarter as they attempted to recover from Banner.

During the first week of January 2010, Geoffrey met with Paul and his Russian friend, whose name was Oleg. He explained the situation, including the chained-up offices that Stephen had found, and he gave Oleg the contact information he had for Gerhard. Oleg listened quietly, and then he said simply, "I will find this man. I will be in touch." Geoffrey left the meeting feeling he had done all he could to deal with Gerhard and that it was time to concentrate on saving his company.

Deep down, Geoffrey was worried that this could be a fatal blow to PMI. PMI's resources and Geoffrey's personal financial situation were both dismal, and the U.K. seemed headed for a double-dip recession.

PMI received some payments in February, which eased the crisis a little. Then Geoffrey went to the U.S. to meet some friends, which turned out to be great therapy and helped him to clear his mind, to renew his faith in mankind and to feel capable of starting the work of rebuilding his personal and professional life.

He knew that he would have to rethink the direction for PMI. Both the situation with Banner and the earlier situation with Jeremy had made it painfully clear that some clients do not pay their fees, even if they have an agreement. He decided that PMI needed to remake itself by cutting staffing and becoming a leaner company that focused on business support, creating value from the pre-planning and supporting companies through phasing of readiness for joint ventures, strategic partnership and importantly growth and investment.

Geoffrey felt it was fairly obvious that this area of operation was most profitable and would put PMI further up the value chain. Geoffrey knew that changes were called for, but he was not sure what internal resources the company would need to be effective with the new strategy – and what these resources would cost. As he traveled back to London from his visit with his American friends, he felt as if he were in the middle of an important game of chess; with his next move, he needed to make significant changes to his company, not only to recoup some of the original investment but also to allow it to continue as a profitable and growing enterprise.

He considered seeking some outside investment of money and skills. He had an associate in Leeds named Harvey who owned several businesses and an investment bank in Switzerland. Harvey and Geoffrey had worked together successfully, particularly in the area of mergers and acquisitions. Geoffrey called Harvey to explain some of the difficulties of the last year. He also told Harvey that he felt that some of the difficulties were because of a pricing model and contractual arrangements that had existed in the past but might no longer be sustainable. Geoffrey said he thought the new business realities were forcing change because small and boutique companies had become too strongly reliant on operating in a cash economy – which had not existed in the U.K. for many decades,

Harvey agreed, and asked Geoffrey what he had planned. Geoffrey replied, "The point where I am currently is putting consultancy services to one side to see how the market improves with time across clients actually paying fees. Meanwhile, I plan to move PMI up the value chain and concentrate on business planning and support services across mergers and acquisitions, pre-IPO, joint ventures, strategic partnerships and capital-raising activities for growth. With these services, we can charge up-front fees and thus maintain our model."

Harvey saw the wisdom of this plan and asked how he could help. Geoffrey replied that he was looking for someone to invest in PMI. The investment would be small; he needed cash flow for three months.

Then he said, "What I am really looking for is a business partner who can add an expert view and provide value by opening new sales opportunities and new ideas. Do you know anyone?"

Harvey said he would think about the proposition and get back to Geoffrey within a week. While he waited, Geoffrey implemented changes in PMI, including reducing staff and moving to more of an associate model.

Harvey called back as promised, and he gave Geoffrey contact information for some people who might be interested in investing in PMI. Geoffrey thanked him profusely, and spent the next few days connecting with the people on Harvey's list. He narrowed it down to two potential investors. One, Daniel, was a successful and self-made entrepreneur who totally understood marketing and business; he was a no-nonsense man with a great attention to detail, and Geoffrey liked him immediately. Daniel and Geoffrey met several times. Daniel asked very detailed questions about the business, how it started, its vision and strategy, its revenues, its failures and successes, and its prospects. It was clear that Daniel could add much to PMI.

While the discussions with Daniel were ongoing, Geoffrey continued to look for business and won several contracts under the new model of paid upfront fees that enabled PMI to stay afloat and even build momentum. After three months, Daniel agreed to invest and take an active role in PMI – a decision that worked out well for everyone.

A PMI client called SBA, which was in the field of renewable technology, asked Geoffrey to accompany SBA representatives to Pakistan to meet with and make presentations to the ministry of agriculture, and the atomic and energy ministry. The trip went well, and when Geoffrey returned to London on 22 August, he discovered he had a message from Oleg, who said he had located Gerhard. Geoffrey returned the call, and Oleg gave him a phone number for Gerhard.

Geoffrey was not sure what to do with this information, but after waiting a few days, he called the number. Gerhard answered, and Geoffrey told the man that he wanted to be paid. Gerhard asked for another week. But of course, he disappeared again without paying.

Geoffrey decided to let the matter go. He was tired of worrying about Gerhard, and he thought the negative energy was not productive. It was time to move on, to focus on the positives, and to reclaim his business. He was pleased with the way the company was evolving, and he was proud of having survived such a painful and damaging experience. He knew that, despite what happened with Banner, he still believed in the original idea behind PMI: The best approach is to act honorably and ethically, and ultimately that will bring success and happiness.

Epilogue

Geoffrey is still a senior partner in PMI, which he has built into an advisory group that specializes in supporting companies through capital-raise activities and investor readiness. PMI has touched more than 200 companies over the last five years.

Recently, as Geoffrey sat in an Italian coffee house on the south bank of the Thames, he thought about those years. He had experienced the highest of highs and the lowest of lows, and he knew he had been tested in ways he had never expected. And yet, he had prevailed. Despite the frustration, anger and fear, he had created a company that fulfilled his vision, he had kept that company alive against all odds, and he had moved it to a point where it was thriving.

He also had learned a lot about himself. He had been forced to recognize his own weaknesses and eccentricities, and he had discovered reserves of strength that he had not known he had. In the process, he had become less judgmental and more accepting of himself and of others.

He realized that leadership forces you to stay true to yourself and to recognize when you are at your best and when you are at your worst; the important thing is to stay focused and keep moving forward. He learned that it is overcoming adversity that brings the most satisfaction, and that achievements are made more meaningful by the struggle it took to achieve them.

Geoffrey felt that he had learned through the ups and downs of his personal and professional life that anything is possible if you believe in yourself and if you set your mind and heart to it. If you want something badly enough, you must be prepared to go after it with everything you have, no matter what the odds.

The important thing is to decide what you really want. On the beach in Grand Cayman, Geoffrey envisioned a different kind of company, one in which there were shared values and shared dreams. Although there were problems to be solved along the way, he persevered and created that company.

Geoffrey had learned more about himself by being put into adverse circumstances than he could ever have learned about himself from a psychometric test or a new Oxford business book; it was reserves of inner self and energy that made the journey possible.

Change has a funny habit of teaching you much about yourself; it goes to the core of your own weaknesses, strengths and eccentricities. Leadership forces you to stay true to yourself and recognize times when you are at your best and worst; the key is to stay focused and to make decisions that will look at continuous improvement. Even though this may be small, incremental change, it is positive change you can build upon even though you may be in quicksand.

PMI taught Geoffrey much about life, learning and sharing knowledge and life stories with his employees and associates. His hopes, fears, beliefs, values and dreams were tested to the limit. He learned that only the difficult things in life truly bring satisfaction, and that achievement is proportional to the struggle needed to get there.

Finally, after everything that Geoffrey had conquered, the most profound truth of his journey was that drive, determination, imagination and energy will bring you success. The question is, how much do you truly want your dream?

He had no idea what the future might hold, but he was glad that he had followed his dreams. As he sat sipping his coffee, Geoffrey recalled the words of Winston Churchill: "This is not the end. It is not even the beginning of the end. But it is, perhaps, the end of the beginning."

About PMI

PMI is a London-based, international strategic consultancy with keen entrepreneurial thinking based around a team of highly successful people. We bring fresh, objective eyes to your business, offering a wealth of business foresight and keen insight. Our experience in research and analysis, strategy and planning, process development, business communications and performance management can bring immense benefits to any ambitious business.

We typically work with companies with turnovers between £250K to £5 million who are looking to position their business for investment and growth. We do this by helping them tackle a range of business challenges including sales, marketing, strategy, business planning and improvement, capital raise activities, M&A, pre-IPO, business integration, risk management and performance
management.

Our track record includes working on challenges within SMEs as well as some of the premium lead Fortune 500 client organisations, delivering integrated people solutions and effective business processes.

Our integrated approach means that we take time to understand each client's business in depth. Only by doing this can we develop an improvement process that meets both their present and future needs. Our solutions impact business performance, employee motivation and customer behaviour.

PMI Consulting Limited
40 Gracechurch Street
London EC3V 0BT
United Kingdom
Email: gsearle@pmi-consult.com
Twitter: @geoffhsearle
Linkedin: http://www.linkedin.com/in/geoffsearle
Website PMI: http://www.pmi-consult.com
Website HSI: http://www.hsbusinessmanagement.com
Blog: http://www.freedomafterthesharks.wordpress.com

About Geoffrey Hudson-Searle

eoff is an international director and strategist with over 18 years of experience in the business and management arena. He lectures regularly on the principles of integrated strategy at worldwide forums, and he is a member and fellow of the Institute of Directors (IOD) and an Associate of The Chartered Institute of Management (CIM). He holds a Master's in Business Administration degree.

Geoff has vast international experience working for major multinational companies and also working as a consultant with a wide range of clients, including the British government, HP, Compaq, BT, Powergen, Intel, ARM, Watsila Group, Atari, Barclays Bank, Societe Generale, Western Union, Chase and Volvo. His areas of expertise lie in brand strategy, business communications, investment transactions, business integration, business improvement and M&A, and pre-IPO; he uses these strengths to strengthen global companies and to develop international business and marketing strategies. He lives in London.

Praise for this book from Amazon.co.uk

***** Inspiring read for entrepreneurs

If you've ever started your own business or are thinking about it, Geoffrey Hudson-Searle's book will inspire you to keep plugging through the challenges that face every entrepreneur.

***** A Reality Check for would be Entrepreneurs

There are too many people who blame a poor start on problems in later life. This book shows how early years adversity can be turned around, that success is earned and that it needs constant graft and expertise to keep it flowing. A very readable, honest and enjoyable book.

***** EXCELLENT!
Excellent and easy reading!
Definitely self inspirational, self motivational with the happy ending life story.
Great book for everyone!
Try yourself…

***** An encouraging life and business story

A well-written and easy to read book about real lives and business.

Take it on a holiday or business trip!

***** An Impressive book!

A true self analysis and evaluation was courageously demonstrated in the book. The book was interesting, meaningful and full of inspirations. It is a SELF JOURNEY that you positively highlighted. Congratulations!

***** Discover the secret to succeeding in your business life

The read of Geoffrey's experiences is one that we see in SME businesses whether we admit to it or not, the book describes how irrespective of what background or circumstance you can succeed, the question whether you admit to or not is how much do you want to succeed. Life, career and setting up your own business takes courage, guts, drive and determination, a great read for those people in any walk of life considering change or transformation in their life, it delivers the tools, what to do and what not to do, but importantly has a good read to take you on the journey with an inspired ending, highly energized read for the serious entrepreneur.

***** stars *Freedom After the Sharks* is written by man who knows all about Sharks!

I like the refreshing openness and knowledge. Written by a City man through and through who tells you exactly how it is in business and how to get through tough times while still being investor ready and making money. A must for all those in business.

***** A deeply inspiring read

With a new author, one never knows what to expect. This is probably one of the most deeply moving books I think I have ever had the pleasure of reading and I have been completely blown away by the incredibly inspiring story contained within. Only half an hour into the story, one begins to connect with the main character Geoffrey in such a way that one is almost moved to tears, knowing all the while that it is a true story. I wanted to scoop the little boy up and take him away from the sorrow that was his childhood after he gets battered again and again. Then there is a beautiful shift and the sad story turns into one of great resolution. I became deeply touched by Geoffrey's determination to make something of his life and his perseverance throughout the many challenges he faced. As the plot unfolds, a great tale of forgiveness and the strength and freedom that comes from that forgiveness is a great message for us all to take away with us. I don't usually write reviews for my books but I felt compelled to do so as never before has a book made me want to get up and make the most of my life as Freedom from the Sharks. This is a great read of how the hardships this little boy faced created a role model to inspire us all. A truly great read.

***** Stellar Blueprint for Entrepreneurship

A lot of books on business aim to cover the principles that led a business man to make a decision. There are books out there that leave you wanting to know more about the protagonist. Then there are books like *Freedom After the Sharks*. This book not only gives you a step-by-step account of Geoff's life, but it shows you what specifically led to his success and failures. One can always ask to know more about what makes a person successful, but Geoff is able to show us a perfect example of what a real book-based road map is.

Life isn't always business, as he shows, but when it is...you get an in-depth look at what it takes to transform a corporation into a high-growth enterprise. It's easy to find 100 different recipes for Apple Pie, but there are very few great books on the step-by-step accounts of how to move a business.

The mixture of personal trials and professional failures will help any reader understand what others have gone through to gain success. This is one of the most connecting books and one can't help but feel empathetic because we too have had our trials and errors. You feel the connection, then you get the blueprints for success as shown by Geoff and PMI.

***** Fantastic, inspiring read. Inspirational

Freedom After the Sharks, an inspiring read of a young entrepreneurs journey to success and how his vision, self-leadership skills, heart and personal code of ethics enabled him to overcome the many personal and business challenges and tests which showed up along the way. Geoffrey Hudson-Searle rises to this challenge with great skill in his accomplished, honest and thoughtful novel – a must read for any budding entrepreneur or business-person.

***** Highly recommended !This really is a great read!

Really enjoyed this book its a really good honest read and I can't recommend it enough. Looking forward to the next book !

***** Amazing book! Brilliant author!

I would most definitely recommend this book, it is a wonderfully well written story!

Very inspiring, it shows that in spite of all adversities one can have a successful career and a fulfilling life!

**** Great book about 'real life'

Too often you read books only about the great business successes of our time. But for every one of the great businesses out there about 1000 fail. This books takes you on a journey that most entrepreneurs take whether they admit it or not.

Nice read.

***** A must read for all budding entrepreneurs

This is not a ordinary read, it is a bible for those who are or want to be entrepreneurs.

We hear few success stories but there are millions of unheard stories of failures too. The author takes us through ups and downs of the mission of being an entrepreneur. It not only can help us understand what not to do but also tells us what to do.

Style of writing is very fresh and looks like a lot of research and personal experiences are the key ingredients.